HARDHEADED WEATHER

Cornelius Eady

Hardheaded Weather

NEW AND SELECTED POEMS

A MARIAN WOOD BOOK

Published by G. P. Putnam's Sons
a member of
Penguin Group (USA) Inc.
New York

A MARIAN WOOD BOOK
Published by G. P. Putnam's Sons
Publishers Since 1838
a member of the Penguin Group
Penguin Group (USA) Inc., 375 Hudson Street, New York, New York 10014,
USA • Penguin Group (Canada), 90 Eglinton Avenue East, Suite 700, Toronto,
Ontario M4P 2Y3, Canada (a division of Pearson Canada Inc.) • Penguin Books Ltd,
80 Strand, London WC2R 0RL, England • Penguin Ireland, 25 St Stephen's Green,
Dublin 2, Ireland (a division of Penguin Books Ltd) • Penguin Group (Australia),
250 Camberwell Road, Camberwell, Victoria 3124, Australia (a division of Pearson
Australia Group Pty Ltd) • Penguin Books India Pvt Ltd, 11 Community Centre,
Panchsheel Park, New Delhi–110 017, India • Penguin Group (NZ), 67 Apollo Drive,
Rosedale, North Shore 0632, New Zealand (a division of Pearson New Zealand Ltd)
• Penguin Books (South Africa) (Pty) Ltd, 24 Sturdee Avenue, Rosebank,
Johannesburg 2196, South Africa

Penguin Books Ltd, Registered Offices:
80 Strand, London WC2R 0RL, England

Some poems in this collection previously appeared in the following volumes, some in
slightly different form: *The Gathering of My Name* (1991), *The Autobiography of a Jukebox*
(1997, reprinted as a Carnegie Mellon Classic Contemporary in 2007), *Victims of the
Latest Dance Craze* (first published by Ommation Press in 1986; reprinted as a Carnegie
Mellon Classic Contemporary in 1997), and *You Don't Miss Your Water* (first published
by Henry Holt in 1995; reprinted as a Carnegie Mellon Classic Contemporary in 2004).
They are reprinted with permission of Carnegie Mellon University Press. Other poems
appeared, again in slightly different form, in *Boom, Boom, Boom* (State Street Press,
1988).

ISBN 978-0-399-15485-0 (hardcover)
ISBN 978-0-399-15511-6 (paperback)

Printed in the United States of America
1   3   5   7   9   10   8   6   4   2

BOOK DESIGN BY AMANDA DEWEY

ACKNOWLEDGMENTS

Some of the poems in *Hardheaded Weather* have been published previously, in the periodicals listed below, sometimes in different versions.

The American Scholar: "How to Do," "John Henry's Hammer"

Callaloo: "Almost Grown," "Santa Claus (come straight to the ghetto)"

Harper's Magazine: "Sherbet," "Victims of the Latest Dance Craze"

Indiana Review: "The Later Songs of Billie Holiday," "Manchild"

The New Yorker: "Cairo, NY," "Handymen"

Ploughshares: "How I Got Born," "My Heart," "Sightings," "Who Am I?," "The Wrong Street"

TriQuarterly (ed. Kimiko Hahn): "The Ghost, the Mountain"

Water~Stone Review: "Nina's Blues"

The Washington Post ("Poet's Choice," ed. Robert Hass): "A Little Bit of Soap," "One Kind Favor"

Thanks also to the journals where some of the older poems first appeared: *About . . . Time, Callaloo, Contact II, Crazyhorse, The Forerunner, The Greenfield Review, Harper's Magazine, Hubbub, The Lake Superior Review, New Letters, Obsidian II, Pequod, Ploughshares, Poet Lore, Poetry Now, Salome, Seneca Review, Seven Stars, Some Things Make Us Strong, Sound and Fury, Survivor, Tightrope,* and *The William and Mary Review.*

"Nature Poem" originally appeared in *Poems for a Small Planet: Contemporary American Nature Poetry,* edited by Robert Pack and Jay Parini (Middlebury College Press/University Press of New England, 1993).

The poems "Leadbelly," "Muddy Waters & the Chicago Blues," "Sherbet," "Song," "The Supremes," "Thelonious Monk," and "William Carlos Williams" originally appeared in the chapbook *Boom, Boom, Boom* (State Street Press, 1988). Sincere thanks to Judith Kitchen and Stan Rubin.

The Modern World was a manuscript scheduled for publication in 1981 by Downtown Poets Press, before the press ran out of funding. Among the poems in it, "Atomic Prayer," "Living with Genius," and "White Socks" later appeared in the chapbook *Boom, Boom, Boom* and in *The Gathering of My Name,* as did the poem "Insomnia." "Charlie Chaplin Impersonates a Poet" later appeared in *The Autobiography of a Jukebox.*

FOR SARAH MICKLEM

FOR ALL MY FAMILIES, BORN AND CHOSEN

FOR PATRICIA AND PETER FILLINGHAM
WHO WALKED BACK INTO THE ROOM

Make it new.

—EZRA POUND

Make it funky.

—JAMES BROWN

CONTENTS

Lucky House

From *Kartunes*

(1980)

From *The Modern World*
(unpublished manuscript, 1981)

From *Victims of the Latest Dance Craze*
(1986)

From *The Gathering of My Name*

(1991)

From *Brutal Imagination*

(2001)

• • •   *This symbol is used to indicate a space between stanzas whenever such space is lost in pagination.*

HARDHEADED WEATHER

Lucky House

NEW POEMS

(1999–2007)

Lucky House

The White Couch

That I found on the curb,
A door or two down from
The New School,
In New York,

Just at the moment
My wife and I were
Looking for furniture
For our new house.

This is how marriage
Works: Guy and gal fall
In love; gal moves
In.

The bachelor pad
With the clean, white
IKEA sofa
Is out.

This is the way marriage
Works: Guy and gal
Buy house,
Guy and gal fight
Over what should
Go in it,

Both problems
Get settled
In the street.

. . .

I sit on the couch.
The couch is mine.
I grab my cell phone.
I call my wife at work.

I found a couch.
I cannot move, or
We lose the couch.
The couch is perfect!
(The couch is free.)

I wait for Sarah.
I guard the couch.
Don't touch the couch.
Don't *consider* the couch.

And now it starts to rain.
I will not move from the couch.
And now the sun goes down.
I will not budge from the couch.

Sarah arrives.
The couch is perfect!
(The couch is free.)

We guard the couch.
We are too weak
To lift the couch.
We are too few
To carry the couch.

. . .

We fear the rain
Will soak the couch.
We are on the couch,

But let's be real!
It's New York City.
We're easy pickings
On the couch.

A truck might roll by
And take the couch.

Maybe we're not meant
To have this couch.
Maybe we're not worthy.
Maybe the Greek gods

Are having fun with us:
Look at them! Fools!
They will not budge
From the couch. Then
The torrent, the East
Village skinhead, the
Cops.

We need a car
To carry the couch.
We need some ropes
To tie down the couch.
. . .

One of us
Must leave the couch.
One of us
Must guard the couch.

I am the one
Who leaves the couch.
I am the one
Who looks for Sarah's mom,

Who gives me her key,
Who lends us her car.

I am the one
Who walks the streets
Searching for rope.
Anyone who thinks
New York never sleeps

Should search for rope
After 9 p.m. I drift
From grocery
To magazine shop.

What do they think
I'm after? My friend, I need
Something
Heavier than twine,

I examine package
After package
Like a wine snob:

Too thin! Too short!
Not enough heft!

Maybe they grunt
At what I choose,
And wait for the headline
Tomorrow: Oh! Yeah! *That* guy!
Weird fuck.

Night has fallen
On the couch.
Rain is falling
On the couch.
My wife is sitting
On the couch.

What will happen next?
How shall we lift
The couch?
How will we tie down
The couch?

How far will the couch go
Before it slips its strings
And flies, stonelike
To the road?

And who shall lie beneath
The couch,
And who shall sue us
For this couch?
. . .

This is when
The doorman arrives.
He's watched us find and guard
The couch.
He's watched us find a car
To carry the couch.
He sees us

As we try to lift the couch.
This is where
The doorman arrives,

Like the woodchopper
Who breaks down the door
And saves the red-hooded
Child,
Like the wand in the cartoon
Witch's hand that
Changes time, space, luck.

This is the man
Who has the rope.
This is the man
Who brings his muscles,

And the couch is lifted
To the roof
Of the tiny Chevy,
And his rope becomes
A tight fist of knots,

And he tells us the story
Of how the couch landed

On the curb, just before
I walked by, and how this
Happens all the time
In the ex–East bloc country
He comes from.

All this moving, he says.
Ah! he says.
This is living,
This is life.

Honeymoon

It isn't until the ink is dry on the contract,
The mortgage has flown to the bank,
That we notice that the John Birch Society
Has adopted our section of the highway.

My sister-in-law
Was right: As soon as the glow
Fades from the lover's eyes,
The farts and hair rollers appear.

Please don't buy it,
She said.
You can't grow plants in rocky soil,
She said.
You can't drive up a snow-slick driveway
In a two-wheel drive,
She said.

You can't allow your concrete back steps
To push slow into the basement,
She said.
All this, plus time and money,

And the in-laws: frost, damp, mold,
Rot, drip, rust.

Mysterious, isn't it?
A turn of light
Above some stumpy
Mountain,
The way a screen porch
Frames a bunch of haggard trees,
The way we squint

At what we love.

Cairo, NY

The town near our house
Isn't fancy, but it is ripe.
At present, it is still on
The wrong side of
The Hudson River,

But there's potential.
What happened
In Woodstock,

What happened
In Red Hook,
What's happening
In Catskill,

Could easily
Happen here.

Our streets are sad
In the way our bodies
Are sad as we
Dream of our
Beautiful selves,

Floating, light,
Light-filled,
Transcendent.

How could anyone
Have missed or
Overlooked us,

Even with our
Bad haircuts,
Our paunchy clothes,
Our gin-mill
Mouths?

One day
Some car drives by
And the rich folk
Who hunt for

Cut-rate rubies
Slow down,

And here we are,
They think,
All ready to be
Scrubbed.

First Nights

The first days
in the new house,
you learn:

(1)
The house
doesn't love
you,
the house
doesn't hate
you

(2)
With little
of your
stuff
in it yet
. . .

The house
looks
a bit like
a shabby
motel

(3)
There is
a grumble
and a
hard click

called a
Sump Pump,

which does,
What?
When?
Why?

(4)
Under the bedroom
floor

There is
a long
rumble,
a small
explosion
every 20 minutes
called a furnace.
. . .

You two,
the Adventure
Team,

Who thought
"quaint,"
but face
"tiny,"

Who just realized
you've bought
a maze of pipes,
enough electrical
wiring to string up
Frankenstein,

Who are known
to the cable guy,
the phone man,
in the bank,
at the
grocery,

As the folks
who finally bought
"the old _____s'
place"!

Hold hands,
shaky couple,
waltz through
the fine print.

Handymen

The furnace wheezes like a drenched lung.
You can't fix it.
The toilet babbles like a speed freak.
You can't fix it.
The fuse box is a nest of rattlers.
You can't fix it.
The screens yawn the bees through.
Your fingers are dumb against the hammer.
Your eyes can't tell plumb from plums.
The frost heaves against the doorjambs,
The ice turns the power lines to brittle candy.
No one told you about how things pop and fizzle,
No one schooled you in spare parts.
That's what the guy says but doesn't say
As he tosses his lingo at your apartment-dweller ears,
A bit bemused, a touch impatient,
After the spring melt has wrecked something, stopped something,
After the hard wind has lifted something away,
After the mystery has plugged the pipes,
That rattle coughs up something sinister.
An easy fix, but not for you.
It's different when you own it,
When it's yours, he says as the meter runs,
Then smiles like an adult.

The Hammer

I still don't know
What to do
With the hammer.

In my hands,
It feels like
My tongue,
Looking for

The right way
To say *please*,
Or *don't shoot*
In, say, French,
Or Swahili:

Best not
To get yourself
In that sort
Of situation
To begin
With,

But my wife
And I,
We bought
This house,

And things
Break,
And things
Fall away

From other
Things,

And so,
The fixing:
The hook,
The nail,

The painting
That might
Dazzle
That corner
Of the wall,

The beautiful
Chair
That could
Be saved.

Don't I wish
I could hear
My father, now

To finish a
Conversation
We never
Began.

What we used
To think
We were
Owed.
. . .

I don't know
How to work
The hammer,

So the hammer
Misses the
Nail, scuffs
The wall,

So the hammer
Hits the nail
A glancing
Blow,

And it bends
The nail
Away from its
True purpose,

So the hammer
Hits the
Thumb.

This is why
This house
Is filled with
Hesitation,

And slow
To mend.

Migration

When we tell a friend in
New York that we've bought
A weekend place, she thinks,
Then tells us how everyone
Is doing this now, after
The fall of the towers,

And I think in self-defense,
But don't say, how the
Towers went down
On a picture-perfect
Workday morning,
After which

All the roads, bridges,
And tunnels were
Shut down, so—
So much for second
Mortgages, baby,
If it happens again.

I don't say this,
Because I know she means
The option to be
Somewhere else,
Because I know she means
The dice, and how we
Get to roll it,

Unlike my parents,
Who headed

North, for jobs,
For houses,
Simply because
Indifference
Was better than
"Never,"

Unlike my sister
And my niece,
Each in their
Gray, sometimes
Bullet-pocked
Subsidized
Apartment blocks,

Unlike my old
Neighborhood,
A maze of
Trying
You're not supposed
To wriggle
Out of,

I hold my tongue
Because we just told our friend
We've bought a house
That doesn't need
To be,

And luck is
So unfair,
Complicated,
True.

Recycling

At the dump, this old hipster/biker takes one look at us,
A middle-aged black and white couple,
Pulling up in their run-down
10-plus-year-old Saturn,
Dutifully lugging the first few weeks
Of meals and mistakes at our new house,
And knows.

It's mid-December; bare branches
Crisscross the horizon,
The air begs to build its first charge
Of serious snow. We are learning
The ways we're expected to deal with
Accumulation.

We haul the coffee grounds
And spent drafts
Fifteen miles from our front door.

He works in a world
Where all the prettiness has long
Been scrubbed away,

And all that's left is what we've done.

To leave our mess behind,
He must punch the ticket we bought
From the county,
We must sort our life
Into those rusting bins.

. . .

Anyone with eyes can tell
We're a story that couldn't have
Originated around these parts. Like him,
We're members of that weird tribe
Of odds and ends,

Tumble seeds that dig in
Where least expected.

Finally, he can let loose:
Here comes another fucking war, he says,
Relieved to have found us.
It piles up in his world,
Like it piles up in ours.

Hardheaded Weather

The leaves
Wave off their stems,
As I drive my
Small red car under
This grumpy
November sky
Toward our house upstate.

Fingers of bare branch,
An argument between the wind
And any object the wind decides to push,
. . .

Pelt of sleet, the hardheaded weather,
A limbed landscape, nudged toward sleep.

A year has passed since you died, and you died, and you.
A world absent of you all
Fidgets at the edge of war and misadventure.

   Friends, who'd guess
I'd own doors your hands won't open,
Floors never to carry your tread?

Against the rolled-up glass,
A CD thrums a folk song about dying.

I think of Whitman in the Civil War,
How he cradled the wounded
At the Army field hospitals.
   Long, long I gazed,
He wrote, high and lonesome as a catgut fiddle.

His polite notion of death
Now a kid's thready pulse
Even his kiss can't repair.

I feel my breath verse, this old throat
Croak chorus. I feel
The push and pull of gusts
That buffet the car frame,
Almost a sail, nearly a kite,
That tug

Before you rise.

Pre-War

In mid-November wind off the
    Mountain
An American flag, left behind by the previous owners,
Stutters on the pole.

Fall loosens its grip:
Dead seed and leaf skitter across the grass,
Smoke ghosts up the chimney.

I hear the mid-morning news
As I watch the mid-morning sun
Wash from the needles of the pines,

Our first dust of snow.

The weather tests the weak spots in the sill,
Stoops our stride, thickens our shirts,
Has come to nest.

Outside

Under the cold wafer of moon,
The stars, scattershot over our roof:
The slugs, the worms, the eggs,
The stings, the mandibles, the hunger
For wood, the spit that rots the leaf,
The poison skins, the needle beaks,

The urge for breakage and blood,
A sack of jeweled larvae under the bark,
A rogue seed poised for snow melt.

The time must come; those rookie wings will stiffen
For a breeze, they will hatch and skitter
They will worm and bore
Under the roots, under our clothes,
Everything we own, a prize.

Lucky House

The phone line has gone dead,
But the hot water, after three weeks,
Returns, and against this blizzard
That walks its sloppy walk up the steps
And onto the porch
The lights burn, and the furnace coughs.

All night the snow washes against our house,
Our small house, our lucky house,
Under the bowing trees,
A desk lamp spilling light from my window.

Our House Is Yours

Shreela:

I watch my wife
Carry the garden
You planted
And she loved
Onto our property.
Hoe and spade,
Rake and seed,

Tending like a monk,
In her old ratty clothes,
Which she keeps
Only here,
Clothes for
The rocky soil
And weeds,

For sweat, and guesswork.
There are days
She comes in

Like a boy who's had
A good tussle
In the mud,
Radiant
From argument.

Digging Out

It is nearly January; all day I hear the wind
Sing its rough music, push the rhododendrons,
Which peek from drifts like strands
On an old man's scalp.

After two days of blizzard, the land
Feels almost ready to make amends,
To remember the dots of houses,
The vanity of pavement,
Or perhaps sleep it off.

Here is the shovel, there is the salt,
Your wrists, your shoulders, lean into
Snow piled against your knees.

Under this,
The foxglove, the steps,
The door to the basement,
The roof with its smart new frosty cap.

The Brakes

She had been drifting, my mother,
Drifting and floating
In the ICU for weeks,

And now it appeared
She was near the horizon

Of recovery, about to ride
That wave home,

Strong enough
To risk a weekend
Off, the doctors
Thought,

And we headed
For the cottages,
My wife, niece,
And I, giddy enough

To overpay
For an old,
Funky,
Mis-
matched

Leather chair,
A lousy sail
On the top

Of our Subaru,
Relieved enough
To haul that
Sucker

Four hours
East
On the
Thruway,

. . .

The tarp
Threatening
To slip
The knots,

To jump
With the wind,

To plop it down in
The living room,
A trophy,
Or maybe,

A reward
For our hunches
And patience,

But then
A clot
In her lung,

And she didn't
Die then,
But we were
Having breakfast
On the front porch,

Taking a breather,
When the brakes
Were applied.

. . .

This is as far
As my poor mother
Gets, then she sinks
Slowly through
Almost.

I'd never buy a chair
Like that, said my niece.
But it isn't her
House, is it?

That's the way
It is with homes.

The objects
You map
The floor with,
The stories
You can't fully justify.

The Tenants

Tell us,
At what moment did the deer decide:
Except
For the brief periods
When the lawn guys
Sweep through,
Buzzing and
Trimming,

. . .

Our lawn
Was theirs?
They stalked us,
So patient,
All summer,

While we walked about
Believing the joint
Was ours,

But there's a
Hobo map in
Their heads,
Called *saplings*
And shoots,

That triangulates
With another
Named *no guns*
Here,

And a third,
Easy pickings,

And we pull up
To the house
One evening,

Weeks later,
Just around
Dusk,
. . .

To stumble
Into their kitchen,
Bedroom,
Nursery.

It's dark enough
For our headlights
To mirror
Their eyes,

Light enough
For them
To shoot us
Back a look,

And know
We see it:

The way a deer
Says *ours,*

Before they flag
Those pretty white
Tails,
And shrug off.

Translation

For a second
I forget where
I am, because
I am half awake,
On the bed,
And the door to the
Outside is
Wide open,

And summer
Has gauzed the air,
And the sound of this
Neighbor, trimming
His lemon trees
And vines,

Is so much like
The sound of
The neighbors
In the States,
Whacking the
Lawn.

Saturday: and if
The husbands
Of Italy and
New York State
Could meet,
Mid-chore,

. . .

How much would
They already
Understand
Before they
Were forced
To babble?

Feast

After we got the news
On how snarky my body
Had become,

We were upstate,
Back at the cottages,
Counting down
The days
Until the knife,
The painkillers,
The catheter,

With our good buddy,
Kathleen,
The only one
To love what she saw
When we first showed her
. . .

What we were thinking
Of buying, our most
Frequent guest.

Keep the boy spinning
Seemed to be
The order of the day.
I remember those weeks

Measured in TV and meals.
Instead of writing
(As I'm sure I should have)
That long, pissed poem,

That middle finger,
That last fart
Kiss-off
To the universe,

It was long, lovely drives
To absolutely
Nowhere special.
I won't go into details.
There's nothing of interest
To the general reader.

It was summer, and we ate:
The fresh corn, the bugs,
The long light,
The breeze through
The screened porch,
Even the sorrow.

Test Drive

Did I dream of the front porch
As I lay in the living room
In my New York apartment,
Post-op? No.

I dreamt of walking
From the couch
To the bathroom, after
I dreamt of walking
From the hospital bed

To the chair beside it,
From the chair,
To the door, without
Falling, as one of my nurses
Prophesied:

They go in so strong,
Then, plunk,
Wet-noodle time.

From the door,
To the hallway,
Slow, like some toddler,
Up and down,
Back and forth,

Hello, gravity.
Only after my knees
Recoup their oil,
. . .

My muscles
Remember
Their age
And duty,

My prick and catheter
End their
Weeklong
Bad date,

Do I dream
Of sitting
On that porch,

Hearing the woodpeckers'
Hungry tap, the white
Noise of cars and trucks
Climbing

The road
Up and down
The mountain,

The insult
Of the neighbors'
Buzz saws, leaf
Blowers, smack
Of BB gun,

Sitting there,
Breathing.

Walk

Either the cancer has
Been cut away,

Or it sleeps, tiny,
An unwelcome
Guest deep within
Some fold, too small
For a worried eye
To draw a bead on,

But in any case, it's past time
To walk, and I pull myself
Out of the chair, say
Good-bye to the glue/
Gravity well of writing
(I can't sit long, anyway),

And I hit the streets
In my drawstring pants,
Which feels like walking
The streets in my PJs,

Which makes me feel
Happily non-adult,
As if I were
Given a pass, exempt
From ever having to worry
About fashion again,

. . .

And I call myself
Recovery Boy,
Walking gingerly

Down Bleecker Street,
Weaving in and out of
The crowds, not quite
A tightrope,

And I call myself
Walking Fool,
As I stride out the
Knots from my
Incision on
West 12th Street.

And here I am
Exercising the gravel
On our driveway
Upstate, raising
Dust with
My steps, making
Small mental notes about
The potholes, the
Curve of grade.

Take the tour:
Slap those dogs
Down and up
The drive,
Wave to the neighbors

As they roll past
In their cars,

Wondering what the hell
You've lost.

The Way a Long Dress Turns a Corner

Communion

After the fall of the towers, it's hard to leave our apartments,
Pull our eyes from the television, stuck on instant replay;
    so many angles,
So many lenses, all this work and effort
    just to be told *they're gone.*
Again, then again. How to deal with this invitation, now
    seemingly from
Another planet, to come and read poetry at a downtown bar?

For the first time in my life, poetry feels a bit foolish; the thought
    of a grown man
Reading verse aloud, a half-mile from a mass graveyard,
    the wreck
Of things too numerous to list, a shamble so loud it
    still rattles in
Our astonished brainpans, even after all these weeks,
    and I hear my parents'
Early doubts; what sort of job is this, the words that say
    I love jazz, my
Singing about mice, the things I overhear, then slot
    into stanzas?
After saying *no* to one or two of these,
. . .

Maybe it's the memory of my dead dad, getting up, rolling out,
   can't recall a sick day
On the job, that plops me in the cab, his soft, wordy boy.
   Maybe I'm
Only doing what the sun-burnt grass on our lawn upstate does;
   what doesn't die off
Soon curls slowly toward the light and air, tender, relentless.
   Maybe I need
What the small crowd that gathers here needs, the boom of
   Sekou Sundiata's voice,
Though the sirens remind us, and the streets are spare
   and ghost-lit,
And we still don't know how to put it.

Nina's Blues

Your body, hard vowels
In a soft dress, is still.

What you can't know
Is that after you died
All the black poets
In New York City
Took a deep breath,
And breathed you out;
Dark corners of small clubs,
The silence you left twitching

On the floors of the gigs
You turned your back on,
The balled-up fists of notes
Flung, angry from a keyboard.

You won't be able to hear us
Try to etch what rose
Off your eyes, from your throat.

Out you bleed, not as sweet, or sweaty,
Through our dark fingertips.
We drum *rest*
We drum *thank you*
We drum s*tay*.

The Later Songs of Billie Holiday

Her voice, rough
Trick of will and breath,
Erodes out.
Even knowing
She's beyond all trouble now,
It's a worry
To listen.
The cabaret law, what
Was it? Gone like spats.

Now her trumpet of a throat
Begins to weed.
. . .

She works harder
To convince these notes to stay,
To treat her right.

John Henry's Hammer

From that last spark
I flew a little, then landed,
Hard, still ringing from his grip, followed by
The rest of him. Our dust cooled
The afternoon heat. For a moment, we
Lay, larger than bets or bosses.
Then a part of me was a good man's ghost, part of me
Rose to pound out the next man's wages.

A Small Story That Involves Me

The two guys behind the counter are black,
But the point about Jackie Robinson (says one) is
The man died a lot sooner than he ought:
You know all the shit he swallowed, had
To keep down. And we nod our heads,
It's just the three of us there, and I nod,
Hey, you bet, you better believe, and there
We are, waiting for my card to clear; not friends,
Not strangers.

Dead Man Rides Subway

(The New York Times, 6-15-99)

He lolls, he sways, this lone male sleeper
Minding his business on the B'way local.
Some let him snooze and think they're
　　doing him a favor,
Others wait to see his head startle awake,
His drowsy panic,
Uptown when he meant to be Downtown,
Downtown when he intended to be Up,
And feel a bit cheated when his nap proves
　　to take longer than their stop.
Need I tell you life in New York City
　　is different? Difficult?
There he floats, slightly out of style
From the rest of us.

Manchild

FOR BELL HOOKS

A warning one white friend hisses
To the one standing nearest to me
At an Upper West Side newsstand.
As if my ears
Could not cradle human speech.

This is the birth of a regret:
My surprise of the woman on my right

As I reach to buy a paper.
How her
Where? becomes an *Oh.*
How they grin,
I am a close call, how they grin,
Pickpocket my ease,
How they
Grin, then push off down the street.
Now I have the rest of Saturday.

Who will touch my hand,
Who will take my quarters,
These clots of syntax
Growing cold in the blush of my palm?

How to Do

It embarrasses my niece to think of her mother
Walking the streets with a cart,
Picking up empties
For their deposits,

But my sister knows how to *do,*
Which was all our mother asked of us.
She's learned how to *do,*
Which is both a solution and a test,

So I stand in line with my sister
At the supermarket.

Today's the best day of the week
To bring the bottles in.

It is a poor people's science,
A concept that works until
Someone with power
Notices it works,

And then, it doesn't.
There's at least 15 carts,
At least 10 people in line,

But only one guy
Behind the counter:
Not what's supposed
To happen.

The manager shrugs,
His shoulders when asked.
No rules here,

Points to a sign taped
Above our heads
Which, boiled down,
Says *wait, behave.*

No rules, except for
What's always been:
Do what you gotta do.
. . .

And the poor stiff

Whose job it is to sort the clears
From the greens, the plastics
From the cans, who is short
One or two people this shift,

Who flings my sister's
Stumpy treasure
Into the hamper's
Great, indifferent mouth,

Temporary chief of staff
Of Lotto,

Who's been instructed to keep
The refunds down to
Twelve dollars' worth of
Store credit, no matter
How many empties
Come in,

Maybe he has a favorite song.
Maybe he's a good guy
To have in a pinch.
He's not paid enough to reveal that here.

This, as my mother would say,
Is the way we have to *do*:
Tired as convicts, we inch along,
Shift our weight
On the black,
Sticky carpet,

. . .

Beholden to nobody's luck
But our own.

Nature Poem

Once,
When I lived
In Virginia,

My upstairs neighbor asked
If, at the reading
I was to give,

Would any
Of my new poems
Include a bit
Of the surrounding
Landscape,

And I said to her,
No, I don't write
About that, but

This was
A false statement.
I could have told her
Behind a certain house
In Illinois
. . .

Is the beginnings
Of a prairie.
I loved
The subtle turnings
Of the word
Brown,

I loved
What a
Clumsy movement
Could toss up:
Feathers,
Survival tactics,

Dust
Slanted by
A mid-November's
Light.

And I could have spoken
On behalf of
The New York
Roof gardens in May:
Small tufts
Of spring,

Near-secret outposts
Tucked within
A city's
Agenda.
. . .

I can't tell you why
Certain things make me
Hold my tongue.

I think the conversation
Dwindled
At that point.
Nervous laughter,
Then she walked
Upstairs.

Why wouldn't a poet
Want to broadcast
Such lush noise?
It was spring
In Virginia,
That particular one
A lovely meter.

It was senseless,
And when she missed
The reading,
Didn't I pluck
A stingy blossom?

In the summer of 1999, Joe Wood, a young African-American freelance journalist, disappeared while taking a break from a conference to go bird-watching on Mount Rainier. Joe's writings were concerned mainly with racial identity in the United States, who we are, and the ways we perceive ourselves.

The Ghost, The Mountain

FOR JOE WOOD

Where is he? Now that the woods
    are quiet, and the snow,
April-thawed, has carved a bit
    more from the rocks
Now that the grass has spiked
    underfoot

Where is the young black man
    in his freshly bought
    jacket and his urban shoes,

the city kid who loves birds?

Poetically speaking, in
Heaven, surrounded
By how the world works,
Deep in the noise
Of transformation,

Swimming the way a rock
Strokes through time.

*

Mount Rainier collects its own memories.
Here's a list: Joe Wood is buried here,
And so is a story about Malcolm X.
Joe Wood is buried here,
And so is a notion concerning hip-hop.
Joe Wood is buried here, first black man dead
On the mountain. Joe Wood is buried here,
With maybe the song of the bird he followed
Singing above his head.

*

Whose world is this?

*

A bridge of snow softens and
Your black body falls to the
Swift water,
A rock cops an attitude and
Grabs your heel.
(Over the ridge you fly.)
Your mother worries your black skin
And soft frame draw the loonies
To your side like nectar.
The living can't know what your body
Told you, then, how the roots
Or current tucked you in, how you
Hurt and slept, and what came after.

*

A ranger says: *This ain't Central Park.*
What to do with you?

They'd like you to be any hiker, but the nuances
Won't lie still:
A black man disappears on a perfect afternoon
Into thin, high air; now doubt nibbles into
A slow day's work. They hope spring thaw
Will prove your plain dumb luck.

    *

If a black man falls in a forest?

    *

The tom-tom cries, and the tom-tom laughs.

On a ridge
Your lover buries her earring, her ring,
Her scent to keep you company.

The tom-tom cries, and the tom-tom laughs.

At home
Your mother boxes your things, won't
Eat the fruit you left behind, wonders
How you were evicted.

    *

Where is the young black man?
There is a blues that says
Gone, never coming back.

Where is the young black man?
There is a blues to raise the spirits,
Another to keep them off your door.

. . .

Where is the young black man?
There is a blues that says
Rambling, can't keep still,
But longs for four walls,
And arms that can hold you,
Keep you steady.

Where is the young black man?
There is a blues that howls the way
The wind howls through the trees.

Where is the young black man?
There is a blues that tells us
Somebody doesn't have a home,
Following the engine's high whistle,
Falling to sleep beneath those pines.

From *Kartunes*

(1980)

Discourse of the Young Poet

I want something different.
I want to be fresh.
I want words
To tumble off my lips
Rich enough
To fertilize
The ground.
I want poems
To metamorphose
Into paintings!
Comic strips!
Classic television!
Sweet fruit and
Vegetables!

I'd like to shift things a bit:
Neon lights
On every farmhouse.
Soft jazz
Piped through the nursery school.
A close-up
Of the face of God.
On every television
In the nation.

But first of all:
Money for reading poems.
Above all else,
Money for reading poems.

The Thief

I am here
To steal poems.
Can't you see
My hidden microphone?
Good. At this café
I'm disguised as a painter
Eating a sandwich,
My next-to-last sandwich
With my espresso. Next week
I will arrive as a nervous
Woman
With a wired gardenia
In my hair.

I have a vision:
NO MORE POETRY FOR POETS.
Ladies and Gentlemen:
NO MORE POETRY FOR POETS.
At least
Not while I'm around.
They laughed me out
Of the place
When I started singing *that,*

But as they will see,
Every dog
Has his day.
Of course I'm crazy.
Crazy
And wired for sound.

Testimony of the Drunk
Asleep on the Couch

I would like to tell the guy
Who arranged this party
That it was meticulously done. Yes.
I dream of
Houses in Spain, an
Old man making
Stained-glass windows. I
Am that old man, and I
Am his son, who dreams of
Driving a big black car. I
Am his daughter, who picks
Smooth stones from a stream
Behind the house. I
Am his wife, who shakes him
Shakes him shakes him when
He drinks too much. I
Have beautiful breasts and I
Know how to measure time by the sun. Yes,
It was a delightful party, it
Was the best party I have ever seen. I

Hope he invites me again. I
Will do anything to be invited
Again.

Success

I will stop dreaming now,
Now that I've finally made it.
Outside I can hear the wind
Rustling through the leaves of trees.
I own those trees.

The Van Gogh Variation

He was so drunk, all
He needed
Was the proper
Encouragement. "You see
That woman over there," I
Said, "The one you've
Been eyeing all night? Well,
She goes for handicapped men.
Yes, she likes men without limbs." I

Laid my knife
On the counter
And left. The next day

He showed me the wound. "I
Nearly did it," he said. "It
Would have gone clean through if
The bartender hadn't of
Stopped me. I

Can't drink there anymore." He
Looked at his hand as if
It were a rare,
Exotic bird.

Then he punched me.

The Idiot Falls in Love

A man absentmindedly scratches his crotch
On the street,
Causing another man to
Walk up to him
And yell:
>   You idiot!
>   Get your hands out your pants!
>   Stupid pig,
>   Get off the street!
>   Can't you see
>   You're upsetting this woman?

The idiot smiles at the man's girlfriend
And the unfortunate woman
Smiles back.

Hawker

I put on dog's teeth,
An Afro
With a silver switchblade
Just
Peeking from the top.
Then the loincloth.
I oil my body.
I walk to a street corner
And sell poems
From a paper bag.
Some contain only
One word.
Some are weather reports.
Some
I make up on the spot,
Others
Are for the drivers
Who pass by,
And laugh at me through their rolled-down windows.

I pretend I'm blind
And the right poem
Brings back my sight.
Some poems
Are saxophones,
Which I blow
Like a black-legged bird.
Others are drums,
Which I bang
Each time the crowd's attention

Drifts.
Others are flowers
For romantics who believe
A poem
Is not a poem
Without one.

I sell them
Until
I reach
The black, soundless poem
At the bottom. Then I go home,
Change my clothes
And become
Anyone.

From *The Modern World*

(unpublished manuscript, 1981)

The Professor Tries to Inspire
His Poetry Students

The professor tries his imitation
Of a man bursting with goodwill.
Out of his pocket comes a pipe,
He greets his students at the door with a handshake,
He tries not to ask embarrassing questions,
But his students leave
Thinking he's sexually confused.

The professor arrives the next morning
Ten minutes late and dressed like
A duck. He props himself
Under the arch of the door
And strips himself, feather
By feather. No one
Reacts.

The professor eats his lunch as if he were in
A foreign country.
This is what he says to his french fries:
You want to know the trouble with the world?
I'll tell you the trouble
With the world:

But the french fries might as well be
A baby, sucking its thumb
As it dreams,
Or a lightbulb in
A Frigidaire.
. . .

The professor returns to class early.
Sweeping the feathers off the floor
He gazes out the window.
An elevated train
Curves toward the platform.

He asks the train:
Would you like to know
The trouble with
The world?

But the train stops only long enough
To let a few people off
And a few people on

And it's gone by the time one of his
    students arrives,
Who notices the mustard stain
    on the professor's shirt
And thinks *poor fish*.

As in:
Out of
The water.

Knowledge

Suddenly
Everything begins to make sense.

The professor opens his eyes.
His bedroom is now
A forest.

How did it happen?
And what does he do now?
Perhaps he is still asleep.

Perhaps an error has been made.
Hair begins to return to his little bald spot.

Birds alight on his windowsill
As if awaiting instructions.

He expects a knock at the door,
A debt collector with wings.

This is what happens:
The timer turns the coffee on.
The newspaper hits the front stoop.
A man reads the college basketball scores
Over the clock radio.

This is what happens:
His wife rolls over and gives him a kiss.
The cat paws the door open
                and leaps to the mattress.
The school bus backfires in the street.

. . .

He knows!
His wife's fingers, sleepy and familiar with
The curve of his head,
Stop.

Living with Genius

It's sundown, and we
Find Gertrude Stein sitting
In her parlor at the
Piano. She's about
To give Alice B. Toklas
The night off. Gertrude
Wants to see if
A piano
Can imitate a violet. Gertrude
Wants to be alone
When she does this, suspecting
That what she wants to do

Is insane. The sun
Sets and Alice
Starts to worry
About her boss; what is
This shit about violets,
Violets, violets,
Anyway? Gertrude
Demands a glass of whiskey,
The shades drawn and all

The lights turned off. With
Pleasure, you old
Coot, Alice thinks
To herself. She does
As she's told and
Goes to bed.

Gertrude
Sits in the dark
All night.

In the morning
She starts thinking
About roses.

White Socks

It is important to remember
That there is a place
For everything.

Those white socks
For example.

They were important
Maybe twenty years ago,
But now
They are
An embarrassment.
. . .

This is not meant
To insult you.
Some of my best friends
Have no taste.

Nor am I afraid
To be seen with you:
As you must know by now,
I was born
Without fear.

But listen to reason.
You know
We can't go
Anywhere
With you wearing
White socks.

Let's talk it over.
Let's clean out your dresser
And then
Walk shoulder to shoulder
Into the future.

The Corpse Before the Library
of Knowledge

All the knowledge
In the universe
Is housed
Right here.

If I'd known then
What I know
Now,
I would have spent all my time on earth
Brushing my teeth.

For example,
My eating habits
Had absolutely nothing to do
With my death.

It's well documented.
The problem is
We're too far away.
It takes forever
For the smallest bit of information
To filter down.

If you knew
What I know,
You'd spend your days
Staring at a blank
Television screen,
With a smile
On your lips.

. . .

You'd never worry again.
Of course,
Some folks
Might call you
An idiot.

Charlie Chaplin Impersonates a Poet

The stage is set for imminent disaster.
Here is the little tramp, standing
On a stack of books in order
To reach the microphone, the
Poet he's impersonating somehow
Trussed and mumbling in a
Tweed bundle at his feet.

He opens his mouth: *Tra-la!*
Out come doves, incandescent bulbs,
Plastic roses. *Well, that's that,*
Squirms the young professor who's
Coordinated this.
No more visiting poets!

His department head groans
For the trapdoor. As it
Swings away
. . .

The tramp keeps on as if
Nothing had occurred,
A free arm mimicking
A wing.

Insomnia

You'll never sleep tonight.
Trains will betray you, cars confess
Their destinations,

Whether you like it
Or not.

They want more
Than to be in
Your dreams.

They want to tell you
A story.

They yammer all night and then
The birds take over,
Jeering as only
The well-rested can.

An Uncomfortable Moment with Eve

He may want the apple,
But I'm holding the apple.

How will he know what it
Tastes like
If I don't give him
The apple?

Everybody tells me what to do,
But now I'm holding the apple.

Use your imaginations.
What do I create
By not giving him
The apple?

I know what he's missing.
And you, God, you, Snake,
I know what you're
Waiting for.

He's too frightened to
Pick an apple.
What if I
Throw this apple
Away?

Newborn

Give me a moment
To get my bearings.

This must be the modern world.
At least everything
Is in the right place.

At least everything is moving.
In my last life
Nothing moved.
Everything was pulled
By strings.

Before I forget everything
I'd like to pay homage to the dead.
Before I forget whom to thank
I'd like to thank my peers
Who decided
The world could use
Another beggar.

I know I'm crying
But I'm happy to be here.
Give me a moment
To get used to it all
Again.

U.S. Involvement in "Latin America"

Andrés Segovia
Sits in a small room.

In the next room
The CIA reads ads
To his guitar.

The guitar refuses to submit.

Segovia
Asks for a glass of water.
No, old man,
Only when your guitar
Decides to reason with us
Then you'll get a glass of water.

Segovia
Dreams of blue fish
As he sleeps
In his chair.

Days pass.
The guitar refuses
To speak.

The blue fish
Tells Segovia
Wondrous things.

The CIA
Asks the guitar

To see reason
"If not for yourself,
Then for the sake
Of the old man."

The guitar refuses to budge.

Segovia
Becomes
A blue fish.

The CIA
Holds the guitar
Accountable.

The House of Misfits

Here
We say:
If the clock is broken
Then the clock
Is broken.

There is a niche
For everyone.

The pianist
Who can perform
Only

During summer
Rainstorms.

The dancer
Who only converses
With wolves.

We spend our flat days on the porch.
A few of us give mirrors
A fresh coat
Of paint.
Others
Comb the sky
For signs:

A respite of
Starlings,
Mistaking our
Outstretched hands
For anyone's,

Snow
Transforming
The stumpy front yard.

Amelia Earhart in Paradise

In a way
I'm glad no one
Will ever
Come calling. This
Was worth
Giving up
My wings. This is
What I was
Looking for, anyway.
I hope one day
The world can shrug
Its shoulders and
Forgive.

Perhaps, one day,
In the going from
Here to
There,
A young girl's
Casual eye
Will glance down
On whitecaps,
And dream of
My scarf,

Perhaps, someday,
A mute piece
Of the wreck
Will float back.
. . .

It's good
No one will be able
To follow.
Each day
Here
Pulls me
A little further
Out. Soon
This solitude will
Close like
A scar.

Thomas Edison, Trying to Prevent the Bottling of His Last Breath

Go away. I'm
Dreaming.
Turn off
The light. I'm

Seven years
Old, the
Village idiot
Again. Get
Lost. Turn
Down
The phonograph.

I'll let you
Know

When I want
To hear
From you. I'll

Wire you
By telegram. I'll
Tune you
On the
Radio.

Give them anything
And
They'll ask
For more.

Give them everything
And
They'll ask
For this.

Breath of
Filament,
And lit
City streets,

Breath of
Cellulose,
And dreaming
In light,

Breath of
Humming
Turbines,

. . .

And dear
Shellacked
Voices.

Progress is bottomless,
I'd say if I had the breath.
They lean in.

Atomic Prayer

If the bomb drops
And I'm riding the
Staten Island Ferry,
Give me time to spit in the water.
If the bomb drops
And I'm on top
Of the Empire State Building,
Give me time
To toss a penny
Off the observation deck.
If the bomb drops
And I'm walking down Fifth Avenue
Grant me a loose brick,
A fresh plate-glass window,
Grant us a moment
When there'll be no need
To play it safe.
Give to us the pleasure
Of misdemeanors.

Let each of us do
What we've always
Dreamed of,
But were too polite
To act out.
Let us extract
Our brief revenge,
Spilling and ripping things
We've been taught
Not to handle.
If we're to die before we sleep,
Grant us a moment to uncover
The secrets behind the door marked *Restricted*,
Authorize us to touch what was always held
  just beyond our reach.
Give us a taste
Of the stolen world.

The Revisionist

FOR EVE MERRIAM

I change the
World
By waving
My hand, and
By waving
My hand,
Hey, presto, the
World
Is changed.

. . .

So treat me
Like eggs. You
Have no
Idea
What a fool
Can do.

Water wings
Under
Ophelia's
Dress.

Lilith
And Eve
Comparing notes.

And you,
Watching me
Cut and paste, you
Can't tell
If you're
In or
Out, if
You should
Worry
Or laugh.

Worry.

From *Victims of the Latest Dance Craze*

(1986)

Dance at the Amherst County
Public Library

Fellow poets,
My Brothers and Sisters,
Comrades,
Distinguished guests and visitors,
Yes,
Even the tourists
In their T-shirts and mirrored sunglasses.

Before our attention begins to wander
Let me ask this:
In one hundred years,
No,
Say fifty years,
If, through grand design or fluke
The world still stands
And leads our descendants to this branch library in Amherst, Va.,

Which poets would they find on the shelves?

The answer probably is
They will only find
What I found this afternoon:
Shakespeare
And Paul Laurence Dunbar.

In view of
And in spite of this awful truth
I would still like to leave one or two thoughts behind:

If you are an archaeologist and find these items slipped into
    Mr. Dunbar's *Collected Works*:
        This poem,
        A pair of red laces

Please understand that this was how I defined myself,
A dancing fool who couldn't stay away from words
Even though they brought me nothing but difficulties.
I was better when I danced,
The language of the body so much cleaner.

I was always in jealous awe of the dancers,
Who seemed, to me at least, to be honest animals.
When I danced

I imagined myself a woman,
Because there is no sight more lovely
Than a woman kicking her heels up in a dive.

This is how I wasted my time,
Trying to become the Henry Ford of poetry,
And mass produce a group of words
Into a thing that could shake
And be owned by the entire world.

Naturally, I failed.

Of course, even the failure was a sort of dance.

My friend,
I bequeath to you what I know:
Not the image of a high, glistening city

But the potential in tall grass, flattened
    by a summer's storm.
Not the dance
But the good intentions of a dance.

This was the world I belonged to,
With its symphony of near-misses,
And in its name
And in the names of all those omitted
I dance my small graffiti dance.

April

Suddenly, the legs want a different sort of work.
This is because the eyes look out the window
And the sight is filled with hope.
This is because the eyes look out the window

And the street looks a fraction better than
    the day before.
This is what the eyes tell the legs,
Whose joints become smeared with a fresh sap
That would bud if attached to a different limb.

The legs want a different sort of work.
This is because the ears hear what they've been
    waiting for,
Which cannot be described in words,

But makes the heart beat faster, as if
One had just found money in the street.

The legs want to put on a show for the entire world.
The legs want to reclaim their gracefulness.
This is because the nose at last finds the right scent
And tugs the protesting body onto the dance floor.
This is because the hands, stretching out in boredom
Accidentally brush against the skirts of the world.

November

Everything fails.
God damn this cold
And this static electricity.
Like the leaves,
I have given up.
Words have become a jelly-like substance
At the base of the skull.

It is another thing I haven't
Asked for.
I take what I get,
And what I've got

Is a lawn filled with surrender,
Snake skins,
Shipwrecks,

A porch littered with consequence
And scientific fact.

. . .

This is the gravity dance.
The same thing that draws us together
Has ruined all these dresses.

January

The old man wants to dance
But can't get started.
May I dance with you? Not yet,
Laughs the beautiful girl
As she spins away
In an air-light
Dress.

He'll never catch up.
It's written right here in the script.
It has something to do
With the balance of the world.

If he catches her,
What will he lose?
The general feeling
That some ideals
Are impossible to live with.

But it will go harder on us.
It will be another thing
We can't just quite put our fingers on,

A slight feeling
Of uneasiness,

Something about the color of the sky,
An alien texture to the air.

The old man wants to dance.
Here are the hard facts:
She'll always be
A few steps ahead of him.

Not yet, she laughs.
Pursuing her,
The other months bounce along behind
Like cans
Tied to the honeymoon bumper.

Piano Concert

FOR CAROL RHODES

What I have always wanted
And all I have always wanted
Is to know an object this perfectly,
To hear my body ring against it,

To keep a piece of this afternoon's light
With its blot of notes
Like sugar on my tongue.

. . .

Is that asking too much?
What I see in your hands
As they wing over the keyboard
Seeps into my bones, lightens me.

I'm not so young that I believe
This will do me any good,
This longing my legs have to bounce
This way,

But I am tired of my eyes glazing
When I read,
The sick light that seems to fall
Over everything. What I want now

Is a sustained chord in my belly,
The uncoiling of the secret
Deep within my muscles. What I want now
Is to rise with these notes

And keep rising.

Crows in a Strong Wind

Off go the crows from the roof.
The crows can't hold on.
They might as well
Be perched on an oil slick.
. . .

Such an awkward dance,
These gentlemen
In their spottled-black coats.
Such a tipsy dance,

As if they didn't know where they were.
Such a humorous dance,
As they try to set things right,
As the wind reduces them.

Such a sorrowful dance.
How embarrassing is love
When it goes wrong

In front of everyone.

Jack Johnson Does the Eagle Rock

Perhaps he left the newspaper stand that morning
	dazed, a few pennies lighter,
The illustration of the crippled ocean liner
	with the berth he had the money
But not the skin to buy
Engraving itself
On the portion of the mind reserved for
	lucky breaks.
Perhaps the newsboy, a figure too small to
	bring back,
Actually heard his laugh,
As the SS *Titanic*, sans one prizefighter,

Goes down again all over New York,
Watched his body dance
As his arms lift the ship, now a simple millimeter thick,
    above his head
In the bustling air, lift it up
As though it was meant to happen.

The Dance

When the world ends,
I will be in a red dress.
When the world ends,
I will be in a smoky bar
    on Friday night.
When the world ends,
I will be a thought-cloud.
When the world ends,
I will be steam in a teakettle.
When the world ends,
I will be a sunbeam through
    a lead window,
And I will shake like the
    semis on the interstate,
And I will shake like the tree
    kissed by lightning,
And I will move; the earth will move
    too,
And I will move; the cities will move
    too,

And I will move, with the remains of
   my last paycheck in my pocket.
It will be Friday night,
And I will be in a red dress.
My feet relieved of duty,
My body in free fall,
Loose as a ballerina
   in zero gravity,
Equal at last with feathers
   and dust,
As the world faints and tumbles
   down the stairs,
The jukebox is overtaken at last,
And the cicadas, under the eaves,
   warm up their legs.

Aerial Ballet

I am not done with my falling.
I turn in the air like a fish
Who realizes he is a fish
Somehow in the middle
Of a tragic miracle.
Do you wish to know about the tiny stars?
Very well.
I will tell you about the tiny stars.
I am a tiny star.
My fingers burn in the air.
. . .

Leaving a vapor trail
That might be mistaken for a jet.

I am not done with my falling.
I turn in the air like a rock
That has always dreamed of being
A great, weightless contradiction.
New York at dusk
Is a cluster of tiny grounded stars,
And as I burn toward their heart
A great peace lightens my bones.

I am not done with my falling.
I turn in the air like a snake
Dreaming off a bad meal.
I am dropped from a bird
Beneath a canopy of stars
Which hiss like the campfires I fall toward
That will make who knows what out of
This awkward story.

I am not done with my falling.
I am following my blood,
Which has decided to court the streets of New York in its own
     strange fashion.
I see the moon,
A pale specter of a star,
Softly appear like smoke before a fire,
And as I plunge, the streets forever curl away
Like cellophane beneath a match.

Miss Johnson Dances for the First Time

When Ophelia met the water
It was a gentle tumble of a dance,
A mixed marriage of a dance.
The swans were confused.
She was a contradiction in terms.
She was, simply put, a beautiful death.

Not so with Miss Johnson,
A wheat field of a girl,
Who held her breath
As she cast herself on the dance floor
In a metallic blue dress

At the Grange Hall on Saturday night,
Holding on to a skinny mechanic

Who knew two steps
That could be shown in public.

It was like being pushed off the raft by her father:
The awful moment when the body believes in nothing.
How ridiculous her body looked.

How her brothers loved to remind her:
A wharf rat.
A drowned cow.

When Amelia Earhart met the water,
Assuming, of course, that she met the water,
Did the sea mistake her for a bird
Or flying fish?

. . .

In the awkward moment she belonged to neither sea
    nor air,
Did she move like Miss Johnson moves now,
Bobbing like a buoy at high tide,
Gulping mouthfuls of air
As her legs learn the beat and push,
And her blue dress catches the mechanic's pant leg
Like an undertow?

Johnny Laces Up His Red Shoes

If Fred Astaire had been really smart,
He would have danced like Johnny dances on Friday night
With his brilliant red shoes
That women can detect half a block away.

If Fred Astaire had been all he was cracked up to be,
He would have danced like Johnny dances on Friday night,
On two pools of quicksilver
Painted fire-engine red.

Johnny is lacing up his red shoes.
He is a pizza,
A kiss in the dark.
And as his fingers tie the laces,
He thinks of long, dark hair.

On his bittersweet sofa bed
Johnny is lacing up his red shoes.

And as his fingers tighten the laces,
His work clothes slide deeper
Into the evening shadows.

If Fred Astaire had been serious,
He would have walked through the door of the neighborhood bar
    like Johnny does on Friday night,
Wearing two small volcanoes
That are permitted to erupt for only three nights.

Radio

There is the woman
Who will not listen
To music. There is the man
Who dreams of kissing the lips
Attached to the voice.
There is the singer
Who reinvents the world
In musical notation.
There is the young couple
Who dance slowly on the sidewalk,
As if the rest of the street
Didn't exist.
There is the schoolboy
Whose one possession
Is an electric box
That scrambles the neighborhood.
There is the young girl
Who locks her bedroom door,

And lip-synchs in the mirror.
There is the young beau
Who believes in the songs so much,
He hears them
Even when
He isn't kissing someone.
There is the mother
Who absentmindedly sways to the beat,
But fears the implications
For her daughter.
There is the man
Who carries one in his
Breast pocket,
And pretends it's a Luger.
There are the two young punks
Who lug one into our car
On the stalled D train,
Who, as we tense for the assault,
Tune in a classical music station,
As if this were Saturday night
On another world.

The Good Look

It is like my father,
His legs turning to rubber,
Taking what he believes to be
His last look at our house.
I imagine my mother, his
Crazy wife,

Standing at the front door,
Believing it all an elaborate stunt,
Or peeking through
The living room blinds
Making as small a target
As possible.

He breathes.
The street reels under his feet,
And now he is like an intoxicated dancer,
Luck wheezing out of his mouth,
Propped up by cousins
Leading him to the open maw
Of their car door,

Which becomes
The line that marks
The borders of the world as
    he knows it,
The line that, once crossed,
Is forever denied.

My father
Stops at that portal,
And, though totally mistaken,
Takes a hard look at his house.

Everything the words *so long* were ever
Meant to imply
Is in this look,
A look that, when shown to me later,

Secondhand,
As part of a story with a
Happy ending,

Nevertheless
Raises the ante.

My Mother, If She Had Won
Free Dance Lessons

Would she have been a person
With a completely different outlook on life?
There are times when I visit
And find her settled on a chair
In our dilapidated house,
The neighborhood crazy lady,
Doing what the neighborhood crazy lady is
    supposed to do,
Which is absolutely nothing

And I wonder as we talk our sympathetic talk,
Abandoned in easy dialogue,
I, the son of the crazy lady,
Who crosses easily into her point of view
As if yawning
Or taking off an overcoat.
Each time I visit
I walk back into our lives
. . .

And I wonder, like children who wake up one day
    to find themselves
Abandoned in a world larger than their
    bad dreams,
I wonder as I see my mother sitting there,
Landed to the right-hand window in the living room,
Pausing from time to time in the endless loop
    of our dialogue
To peek for rascals through the
Venetian blinds,

I wonder a small thought.
I walk back into our lives.
Given the opportunity,
How would she have danced?
Would it have been as easily

As we talk to each other now,
The crazy lady
And the crazy lady's son,
As if we were old friends from opposite coasts
Picking up the thread of a long conversation,

Or two ballroom dancers
Who only know
One step?

What would have changed
If the phone had rung like a suitor,
If the invitation had arrived in the mail
Like Jesus, extending a hand?

The Poetic Interpretation of the Twist

I know what you're expecting to hear.
You think to yourself: Here's a guy who must understand what
    the twist was all about.
Look at the knuckles of his hands,
Look at his plain blue shirt hanging out of the back
    of his trousers.
The twist must have been the equivalent of
    the high sign
In the secret cult.

I know
I know
I know

But listen: I am still confused by the miniskirt,
As well as the deep meaning of vinyl on everything.
The twist was just a children's game to us.
I know you expect there ought to be more to this,
The reason the whole world decided to uncouple,

But why should I lie to you? Let me pull up a chair
And in as few words as possible,
Re-create my sister,
Who was renowned for running like a giraffe.
Let me re-create my neighborhood,
A dead-end street next to the railroad tracks.
Let me re-create
My father, who would escape the house by bicycle
And do all the grocery shopping by himself.

. . .

Let's not forget the pool hall and the barbershop,
Each with its strange flavors of men,
And while we're on the subject,
I must not slight the ragweed,
The true rose of the street.

All this will still not give you the twist.

Forgive me for running on like this.
Your question has set an expectation
That is impossible to meet.

Your question has put on my shoulders
A troublesome responsibility

Because the twist is gone.
It is the foundation of a bridge
That has made way for a housing project

And I am sorry to admit
You have come to the wrong person.
I recall the twist
The way we recall meeting a distant aunt as a baby
Or the afternoons spent in homeroom
Waiting for the last bell.

My head hurts.
I am tired of remembering.
Perhaps you can refresh my memory
And tell me
How we got on this topic?
As a favor to me,

Let's not talk anymore about old dances.

I have an entire world on the tip of my tongue.

Jazz Dancer

I have a theory about motion.
I have a theory about the air.
I have a theory about main arteries and bass lines.
I have a theory about Friday night,
Just a theory, mind you,
About a dry mouth and certain kinds of thirst
And a once-a-month bulge of money
    in a working pair of pants.

I have a theory about kisses,
The way a woman draws a man across a dance floor
Like a ship approaching a new world.
I have a theory about space
And what's between the space,

And an idea about words,
A theory about balance and alphabet,
A theory concerning electricity and the tendons,
A hunch about long glances from across a ballroom,
Even though there's a man on her arm,
Even though there's a woman on his arm,

And Fire and the Ocean,
Stars and Earthquakes,
Explosions as sharp as new clothes
    off the rack.

When I leap,

Brushes strike the lip of a cymbal,
When I leap,
A note cuts through glass.
When I leap,

A thick finger dreams on a bass string
And all that sweat,
All that spittle,
All those cigarettes and cheap liquor,

All that lighthearted sass and volcanism,
All that volatile lipstick,
All that

Cleaves the air the way a man and woman
Sweet-talk in a bed.
When I leap,
I briefly see the world as it is
And as it should be

And the street when I grew up,
The saxophones,
Kisses
And mysteries among the houses

And my sister, dressing in front of her mirror,
A secret weapon of sound and motion,
A missionary
In the war against
The obvious.

Victims of the Latest Dance Craze

The streamers choking the main arteries
Of downtown.
The brass band led by a child
From the home for the handicapped.
The old men
Showing their hair (what's left of it),
The buttons of their shirts
Popping in time
To the salsa flooding out
Of their portable headphones.

And mothers letting their babies
Be held by strangers.
And the bus drivers
Taping over their fare boxes
And willing to give directions.

Is there any reason to mention
All the drinks are on the house?
Thick adolescent boys
Dismantle their BB guns.

Here is the world (what's left of it),
In brilliant motion,
The oil slick at the curb
Danced into a thousand
Splintered steps.
The bag ladies toss off their
Garments
To reveal wings.
. . .

"This dance you do," drawls the cop,
"What do you call it?"
We call it scalding the air.
We call it dying with your
Shoes on.

And across the street
The bodies of tramps
Stumble
In a sober language.

And across the street
Shy young girls step behind
Their nameless boyfriends,
Twirling their skirts.

And under an archway
A delivery boy discovers
His body has learned to speak,
And what does this street look like
If not a runway,
A polished wood floor?

From the air,
Insects drawn by the sweat
Alight, when possible,
On the blur
Of torsos.
It is the ride
Of their tiny lives.

The wind that burns their wings,
The heaving, oblivious flesh,

Mountains stuffed with panic,
An ocean
That can't make up its mind,
They drop away
With the scorched taste
Of vertigo.

And under a swinging lightbulb
Some children
Invent a game
With the shadow the bulb makes
And the beat of their hearts.
They call it dust in the mouth.
They call it horse with no rider.
They call it school with empty books.

In the next room
Their mother throws her dress away to chance.
It drops to the floor
The way a brush sighs across a drum head,
And when she takes her lover,
What are they thinking of
If not a ballroom filled with mirrors,
A world where no one has the right
To stumble?

In a parking lot
An old man says this:
"I am a ghost dance.
I remember the way my hair felt
Damp with sweat and wind.

. . .

"When the wind kisses the leaves, I am dancing.
When the subway hits the third rail, I am dancing.
When the barrel goes over Niagara Falls, I am dancing.
Music rings my bones like metal.

"O, Jazz has come from heaven," he says,
And at the *z* he jumps, arching his back like a heron's neck,
And stands suddenly revealed
As a balance demon,
A home for
Stetson hats.

We have all caught the itch:
The neon artist
Wiring up his legs,
The tourist couple
Recording the twist on their
Instamatic camera,
And in a factory
A janitor asks his broom
For a waltz.
And he grasps it like a woman
He'd have to live another
Life to meet,
And he spins around the dustbin
And machines and thinks:
Is everybody happy?
And he spins out the side door,
Avoiding the cracks in the sidewalk,
Grinning as if he'd just received
The deepest kiss in the world.

From *The Gathering*
of My Name

(1991)

The Grin

I saw it
On the mouth of a
Plainclothes cop
At the Norfolk airport.
Running from the gate
To the taxi stand made me his
Business.

A black man, bolting
For an exit, is a
Sweet suspicion.
"Will you cooperate?"
He asked. It wasn't
A question.

That was the first time. When
It happened again, same
Circumstances, same face,
I realized the grin on it,
Barely held in check,

Was his trademark.
He let me go.
"See you soon,"
He said,
           to all of us.

The Wrong Street

If you could shuck your skin and watch
The action from a safe vantage point,
You might find a weird beauty in this,
An egoless moment, but for
These young white men at your back.
Your dilemma is how to stay away from
The three-to-five-second shot
On the evening news of the place
Where you stumble, or they catch
Their second wind, or you run up
To the fence, discover that
You are not breeze, or light,
Or a dream that might argue
Itself through the links. Your responsibility
Is not to fall bankrupt, a
Chalk-marked silhouette faintly
Replaying its amazement to
The folks tuning in, fist to
Back, bullet to midsection.
Your car breaks down
And gives you up. A friend's
Lazy directions miss
The restaurant by two
Important blocks. All of this
Happened. None of this
Happened. Part of this
Happened. (You dream it
After an ordinary day.) Something
Different happened, but now
You run in an

Old story, now you learn
Your name.

Why Do So Few Blacks Study Creative Writing?

Always the same, sweet hurt,
The understanding that settles in the eyes
Sooner or later, at the end of class,
In the silence cooling in the room.
Sooner or later it comes to this,

You stand face-to-face with your
Younger face and you have to answer
A student, a young woman this time,

And you're alone in the classroom
Or in your office, a day or so later,
And she has to know, if all music
Begins equal, why this poem of hers
Needed a passport, a glossary,

A disclaimer. *It was as if I were . . .*
What? Talking for the first time?
Giving yourself up? Away?
There are worlds, and there are worlds,
She reminds you. She needs to know
What's wrong with me? and you want
. . .

To crowbar or spade her hurt
To the air. You want photosynthesis
To break it down to an organic language,
You want to shake *I hear you*
Into her ear, armor her life

With permission. Really, what
Can I say? That if she chooses
To remain here the term
Neighborhood will always have
A foreign stress, that there
Will always be the moment

The small, hard details
Of your life will be made
To circle their wagons?

Song

Nigger-Lover is a song, spat out
Of an open car window
At dusk,

At the great mall in
Lynchburg, Va., the
First time in

Five years we've
Heard it. We
Almost made it,

. . .

Amazed this hasn't
Happened before. It
Was the end of

Our going-away party.
We were walking out
Across the lot. What

Those drunken boys in
The black Chevy saw
Was so obvious. What

Else could they make
Of this invitation?
We almost made it,

Always carried the possibility
With us for years,
But it was

The end of our
Going-away party. Almost,
Almost, almost got out

Scot–free, almost
Didn't have
To hear it

Right where
You are supposed
To hear it, almost

. . .

Didn't have to drive home
Thinking hard about
The headlights

At our backs, carry
Their hard singing
Away in our

Cars, in our heads. We
Almost, almost,
Almost

Got away. We were just
Walking out, soft
Twilight

In the hills surrounding
The lot, laughing
Our plump laughs,

Nearly gone.

Sherbet

The problem here is that
This isn't pretty, the
Sort of thing that

Can easily be dealt with
With words. After
All it's

. . .

A horror story to sit,
A black man with
A white wife in

The middle of a hot
Sunday afternoon in
The Jefferson Hotel in

Richmond, Va., and wait
Like a criminal for service
From a young white waitress

Who has decided that
This looks like something
She doesn't want

To be a part of. What poetry
Could describe the
Perfect angle of

This woman's back as
She walks, just so,
Mapping the room off

Like the end of a
Border dispute, which
Metaphor could turn

The room more perfectly
Into a group of
Islands? And when
. . .

The manager finally
Arrives, what language
Do I use

To translate the nervous
Eye motions, the yawning
Afternoon silence, the

Prayer beneath
His simple inquiries,
The sherbet which

He then brings to the table personally,
Just to be certain
The doubt

Stays on our side
Of the fence? What do
We call the rich,

Sweet taste of
Frozen oranges in
This context? What do

We call a weight that
Doesn't fingerprint,
Won't shift,

And can't explode?

Alabama, c. 1963: A Ballad by John Coltrane

But
Shouldn't this state have a song?
Long, gliding figures of my breath
Of breath
Lost?

Somebody can't sing
Because somebody's gone,
Somebody can't sing
Because somebody's gone.

Shouldn't this landscape
Hold a true anthem?

    What
You can't do?
    Whom
You can't invent?
    Where
You can't stay?
    Why
You won't keep it?

But
Shouldn't this state
Have a song?

And shall we call it
My face will murder me?
And shall we call it

I'm not waiting?

Leadbelly

You can actually hear it in his voice:
Sometimes the only way to discuss it
Is to grip a guitar as if it were
Somebody's throat
And pluck. If there were

A ship off of this planet,
An ark where the blues could show
Its other face,

A street where you could walk,
Just walk without dogged air at
Your heels, at your back, don't
You think he'd choose it?
Meanwhile, here's the tune:
Bad luck, empty pockets,
Trouble walking your way
With his tin ear.

Muddy Waters & the Chicago Blues

This just in from the windy city: Thomas Edison's
Time on the planet has been validated. The guitars
And harps begin their slow translation
Of the street, an SOS of what you need
And what you have. The way this life
Tries to roar you down, you have to fight

Fire with fire: the amplified power
Of a hip rotating in an upstairs flat
Vs. the old indignities; the static
Heat of *nothing, nowhere,*

No how against this conversation
Of fingers and tongues, this
Rent party above the
Slaughterhouse.

Thelonious Monk

I know what to do with math.
Listen to this. It's
Arithmetic, a sound track. The motion

Frozen in these lampposts, it
Can be sung. I can lift away
Its logic, make it spin
. . .

Like an orbital satellite, find
Gambling's true pitch.
It can be *played*:

Adventure, the trying of
Patience, holding back, holding
Up, laying out, stop-time,

Slow motion, time travel,
Spacewalking. It can be
Splintered, strained

Through the fine mesh
Of a second. Now I try
A few bars of *what's next?* Run

It over my hands, ignite it,
Make the fire sound like
April in Paris

William Carlos Williams

Didn't like jazz, he once claimed
In an interview,
The good doctor's reaction to it
A bit like a hand retracting
From a slim volume

Of 20th century verse. In
Other words: Good intentions,
But what does this *yak, yak, yak*

Have to do with me? This,
You understand, from a person
Who listened
To an industrial river, forced
A painter's brush to give up
Its low, animal noise,

Broke trees into
Sense.

The Supremes

We were born to be gray. We went to school,
Sat in rows, ate white bread,
Looked at the floor a lot. In the back
Of our small heads
. . .

A long scream. We did what we could,
And all we could do was
Turn on each other. How the fat kids suffered!
Not even being jolly could save them.

And then there were the anal retentive,
The terrified brown-noses, the desperately
Athletic or popular. This, of course,
Was training. At home

Our parents shook their heads and waited.
We learned of the industrial revolution,
The sectioning of the clock into pie slices.
We drank cokes and twiddled our thumbs. In the
Back of our minds

A long scream. We snapped butts in the showers,
Froze out shy girls on the dance floor,
Pinpointed flaws like radar.
Slowly we understood: this was to be the world.

We were born insurance salesmen and secretaries,
Housewives and short order cooks,
Stockroom boys and repairmen,
And it wouldn't be a bad life, they promised,
In a tone of voice that would force some of us
To reach in self-defense for wigs,
Lipstick,

Sequins.

Gratitude

I'm here
        to tell you
                an old story.
                This
Appears to be
        my work.
                I live
                in the world,
Walk
        the streets
                of New York,
                this
Dear city.
        I want
                to tell you
                I'm 36
Years old,
        I have lived
                in and against
                my blood.
I want to tell you
        I am grateful,
                because
                (after all)
I am a black
        American poet!
                I'm 36,
                and no one

Has to tell me
        about luck.
                I mean:
                after a reading
Someone asked me
        once:
                If
                you weren't
Doing this,
        what
                (if anything)
                would you be doing?
And I didn't say
        what we both
                understood.
                I'm
A black American male.
        I own
                this particular story
                on this particular street
At this particular moment.
        This appears
                to be
                my work.
I'm 36 years old,
        and all I have to do
                is repeat
                what I notice
Over
        and over,
                all I have to do
                is remember.

And to the famous poet
        who thinks
                literature holds
                no small musics:
Love.
        And to the publishers
                who believe
                in their marrow
There's no profit
        on the fringes:
                Love.
                And to those
Who need
        the promise of wind,
                the sound of branches
                stirring
Beneath the line:
        here's
                another environment
                poised
To open.
        Everyone reminds me
                what an amazing
                Odyssey
I'm undertaking,
        as well they should.
                After all,
                I'm a black,
American poet,
        and my greatest weakness
                is an inability
                to sustain rage.

Who knows
            what'll happen next?
                        This appears to be one
                        for the books,
If you
            train your ears
                        for what's
                        unstated
Beneath the congratulations(!)
            That silence
                        is my story,
                        the pure celebration
(And shock)
            of my face
                        defying
                        its gravity,
So to speak.
            I claim
                        this tiny glee
                        not just
For myself,
            but for my parents,
                        who shook their heads.
                        I'm older now
Than my father was
            when he had me,
                        which is no big deal,
                        except
I have personal knowledge
            of the wind
                        that tilts the head back.
                        And I claim

This loose-seed-in-the-air glee
      on behalf of the
      social studies teacher
I had in the tenth grade,
      a real bastard
         who took me aside
         after class
The afternoon
      he heard I was leaving
         for a private school,
         just to let me know
He expected me
      to drown out there,
         that I held the knowledge
         of the drowned man,
The regret
      of ruined flesh
         in my eyes,
         which was fair enough,
Except
      I believe I've been teaching
         far longer now
         than he had that day,
And I know
      the blessing
         of a
         narrow escape.
And I claim
      this rooster-pull-down-morning glee
         on behalf of anyone
         who saw me coming,

And said yes,
     even
          when I was loud, cocky,
          insecure,
Even
     when all they could have seen
          was the promise of a germ,
          even
When it meant
     yielding ground.
          I am a bit older
          than they were
When I walked
     into that room,
          or class,
          or party,
And I understand the value
     of the unstated push.
          A lucky man
          gets to sing
his name.
     I have survived
          long enough
          to tell a bit
Of an old story.
     And to those
          who defend poetry
          against all foreign tongues:
Love.
     And to those who believe
          a dropped clause
          signifies encroachment:

Love.
                And to the bullies who need
                        the musty air of
                        the clubhouse
All to themselves:
                I am a brick in a house
                        that is being built
                        around your house.
I'm 36 years old,
                a black, American poet.
                        Nearly all the things
                        that weren't supposed to occur
Have happened (anyway),
                and I have
                        a natural inability
                        to sustain rage,
Despite
                the evidence.
                        I have proof,
                        and a job that comes
As simple to me
                as breathing.

From *You Don't Miss Your Water*

(1995)

I Know (I'm Losing You)

Have you ever touched your father's back? No, my fingers tell me,
as they try to pull up a similar memory.

There are none. This is a place we have never traveled to,
as I try to lift his weary body onto the bedpan.

I recall a photo of him standing in front of our house. He is
large, healthy, a stocky body in a dark blue suit.

And now his bowels panic, feed his mind phony information,
and as I try to position him, my hands shift, and the news shocks
me more than the sight of his balls.

O, bag of bones, this is all I'll know of his body, the sharp
ridge of spine, the bedsores, the ribs rising up in place like new
islands.

I feel him strain as he pushes, for nothing, feel his fingers
grip my shoulders. *He is slipping to dust,* my hands inform me,
you'd better remember this.

A Little Bit of Soap

One of the things my father never liked about me was my dark
skin. *You used to be so pretty,* was the way he'd put it, and it was
true, there is proof, a baby picture of a curly-haired, just-a-hairs-
breadth-away-from-fair-skinned child, me, my small fingers balled
up into fists.

And then, as if some God shrugged and suddenly turned away
its gaze, something caved in, and I was dark, dark, and all that it
implied.

So what happened? My father always seemed to want me to
explain, what did this desertion mean? This skin that seemed

born to give up, this hair that crinkled to knots, this fairy-tale-like transformation?

You used to look real good, my father, a man of slightly lighter hue, would say to me, his son, his changeling. *Maybe you ought to wash more.*

One Kind Favor

My father is close to death, and in his final hours, he begins his journey by asking anyone within earshot of his bed for a few things.

He asks to be allowed to go back home to Florida.

He asks to be able to cast off his dreary hospital gown, to be reunited to the shape of his own clothes.

He wants someone to fetch him his shoes, now useless for weeks, the impossible act of slipping them on, the slight miracle of bending and tying.

In his wishes, my mother arrives and sits at his bedside, or he changes it, and he walks back into his house, into the living room, his old chair.

He is so close to dreaming now, and his body lifts with the desire to fix things.

Soothe Me

What happened to my money? My father asks me this toward the end of one of my visits to the hospital, and I think he must mean the large wad of cash he loves to flash and carry, the only leverage he thinks an old man has over the world, the thing I love the least about him, skinflint, miser, moneygrubber, tightfisted ruler of the house.

But no, it's smaller; he's talking petty cash.

Look over there in that drawer, he says, *don't you see it?*

I see just what I expect: tongue depressors, baby oil, the diabetic candy he sniffed and left by the side of the road. If there was any cash there, it is long gone, a secret boon for some nurse or orderly, a justifiable tax for a hard-ass patient.

So why don't I tell him the truth? Instead, I reach in my wallet, ask him, *you mean this?* And he watches me as I do, and believes it; he robs me of twenty bucks, and I let him.

I remember the strength left in his fingers, the way they clamped around the bill. If it was a kiss, we'd tease, *who's your girlfriend?* If it was a moment in a song, the lyric would sing, *without you, I'm nothing.*

A Rag, a Bone, and a Hank of Hair

I'm sitting alone with my father at the funeral parlor. Viewing hours have just begun, but it's midday workweek, and for a few hours it'll be just me and him, the first time I've laid eyes on him since the phone call woke me up.

I'm doing what a son is supposed to do, or so I've been told, but it's hard work, sitting with what used to love and trouble you.

Of course, his body is a bright lie in its casket, everything that has brought him here carefully hidden or rearranged.

Is there something I want to tell him? Anything I can forgive?

I can only sit and wait and listen to the gospel music as it buzzes through the speakers. *Jesus, Jesus, Jesus.* All his time, all his struggles that I still call life.

All his trials.

All God's Dangers

The house has gone down, I try to tell my father in the hospital, *it isn't worth that much anymore.*

He won't have any of it, this man who has kept such a shining memory of what he's bought with his hands so close to his heart, so close to what he knows he's made of, that I'm reduced to a bogeyman who happens to wear his son's face.

I tell him he's been overpaying his taxes on it for years, this stingy man who has been forced to go through so many quick changes these last few months.

Mr. Bones is prying my father's hands, finger by finger, away from the things that he knows of this world, and this latest revelation's a major blow, something I can tell is twisting his life into meaningless shapes.

Far better to think his silly boy, the one who earns his living from talking funny, has once again misunderstood the way this world's supposed to work.

Uh-uh! he shoots back, eyes expanding to take in all God's dangers. This is how life, sharpened to a fine point, plunges into what we call hope. This is how death, if it's given enough time, irons out the small details.

Money (That's What I Want)

My father has just died, and now I must stand in line at the Manhattan branch of his bank in order to withdraw funds from his accounts before they find out and freeze them in probate.

My daddy is gone, but if I want to give him a proper burial, I must begin this last dance with him. I must stuff my pockets with his mojo, the greenback dollar, the one true spell he ever believed in, and then walk two awkward blocks from his bank to mine.

The teller takes his time checking me out. He can smell that something isn't quite right, but since my power of attorney is in working order we both know how this transaction must end.

He must count my father's leavings into my hand. How transparent my pockets will feel under the midday New York sun. How nervous my steps as I carry him.

Motherless Children

How many ways do I want to kill this woman, this young bureaucrat at the Office of Social Services, for wanting to kill me? Kill me slowly by degrees, kill me with provisions, kill me in measured words, kill my mother by rubbing her sad life with my father in her face. O, how this woman, bored, dulled by repetition, wants my mother officially rendered inert, reduced to a mere boarder in a broken-down ghetto house, how she wants the word *bastard* to define our conversation.

What did I say or do? Who knows, but I do know this look she's giving me, after telling me that there's no place for my mother's well-being in their guidelines, that as far as they're concerned, she isn't even legally a part of my family. I know this look. This woman wants to observe a screamer, a ripper, she wants her dreams of a babbling monkey to rise.

Blow up, she whispers, as she explains what she isn't going to do for me, how my father's bound to disappear, item by item, first his house, then his cars, then all his money except for what it takes for a pine box and a hole.

She thinks she's the facts of life, a wall with no apparent handholds, the river referred to in the old spirituals: deep, wide, fraught with many sorrows, and her eyes dare me to become a nigger and kick over the table.

Papa Was a Rolling Stone

A few weeks before my father dies, my sister tells me a fuzzy story about a young woman she'd heard rumors about, a class or two ahead of her in high school, who carried our unusual last name.

And when my niece goes through some of my father's papers, she uncovers a small laminated card, a birth certificate from a midwestern state, for a boy, born a year before I was, though it's a different last name.

What about this? We want to know, and we badger my father in the hospital, until he finally admits to us that the woman my sister tried but never got to meet in high school was indeed our half sister.

My father tells us that when my niece was an infant, and my sister was living away in Florida, he'd bundle my niece up and take her to this woman's apartment. He was that proud of being a grandfather, and he knew my niece would be too young to remember.

She married a rich man, and they moved away to Israel, is as far as he's willing to take us on this. *She's happy, and I don't want to bother her.*

And the birth certificate? I see language in the way the bones in his thin body twist; his mouth says, *Beats me.*

He's pissed off that it's come down to this, that his children would have enough time to try and unravel a man's business.

And then he clucked, which I took to mean, *What makes you think I owe you this?*

The Chapel of Love

And now, alas, it is too late. My wife and I are trying to tell my mother how wise it would be for her to finally marry my father, now that he is lying, half a shade, in the hospital.

His doctors feel he'll be dying slow, and he's burning up his pensions. Soon, he will have to go on Medicaid, and the rules are firm. Single men who have made no provisions must sign practically everything over to the Government, must, in their ironic terms, "spend down" to an income they haven't seen since they were starting out, must whittle their desires to small items, chewing gum, haircuts, playing cards; must transform themselves, whether they want it or not, from homeowners to paupers.

Though they've lived together for over forty years, as far as the Government's concerned, without a paper, my mother is simply the woman he's been keeping. If they're not married, and soon, she'll lose the house.

My father tells us he's willing, but when we bring this up with my mother, she answers with the voice I know she had on the day that she finally saw how things were with my father, that they would never wed; the young woman who decided with her last drop of self-worth, that a part of his one good thing had come and gone.

What a cold day that must have been in her heart. She will never visit him in the hospital. And now, in a voice that could damn a saint, she is telling us she'd rather starve on her anger than feed off his slow regret.

I Just Wanna Testify

There was, at the end, a look of great peace on my father's face at the moment of his death. At the memorial service my cousin tells this story to us as a way to infer a last-minute salvation, a meeting of Jesus in the middle of the air, this being, after all, the AME Zionist church across from the vacant lot that used to be the elementary school me and my sister attended.

This is the part of the service where we stand up for him, this small knot of family and friends in a very large room.

He's gone and left my mother with nothing. Her name isn't on the deed to the house, her name never appears on his policies. Her mind's confused, she can't take care of herself by herself, and I'm having a real hard time convincing various agencies that she even exists.

Which is why there is no casket to bear. Too expensive, we decide, money to be better spent on the living, on my mother.

Still, we give him a family send-off. *A hard man, but his own man!* Sing the testimonies. *A stingy man, but a family man!* And I truthfully thank him for the roof he put over our heads, for staying when a lot of other men took a look at their wives, their babies, their house bills and changed their names to fare-thee-well.

And then my sister stands up, stands up through the pain and accidents of first born, first torn, stands up, the family's "bad girl," the willful daughter, low-down spirit of red dresses and iodine, my sister stands up in a way I can't fully explain, but know belongs to black women, she stands up and declares, *I'm just like him, but I'm a woman, so I can't get away with it.*

Deuce and a Quarter

FOR TOM ELLIS

The dust of my father the furnace missed
Is here in his Buick Electra 225
That has been parked, unopened,
In the driveway since his death.
In order to sell it,
We exhume the door to look for papers,

And (surprise) here is his sweat,
Mingled with pitted chrome and wasps' nests.
Bridle with no horse, plow without a field,
Not even the house was his like this.

. . .

And now his death
Is everyday business,
And I am any son
Who must finally remove the plates,
Then phone a truck to pull
This collision away;
A car, like any car.

You Don't Miss Your Water

At home, my mother wakes up and spends some of her day talking
back to my father's empty chair.

In Florida, my sister experiences the occasional dream in which
my father returns; they chat.

He's been dead and gone for a little over a year. How it would
please me to hear his unrecorded voice again, now alive only in
the minds of those who remember him.

If I could, if as in the old spiritual, I could actually get a direct
phone link to the other side, I could call him up, tell him about
this small prize of a week I've had teaching poetry at a ski resort a
few miles from Lake Tahoe, imagination jackpot, brief paradise of
letters.

How could I make him believe that I have gotten all of this,
this modern apartment, this pond in front of my window, all from
the writing of a few good lines of verse, my father, who distrusted
anything he couldn't get his hands on?

Most likely, he would listen, then ask me, as he always did, just
for safety's sake, if my wife still had her good-paying job.

And I can't tell you why, but this afternoon, I wouldn't become hot and stuffy from his concern, think "old fool," and gripe back, *Of course I'm still teaching college. It's summer, you know?*

This afternoon, I miss his difficult waters. And when he'd ask, as he always would, *How're they treating you?* I'd love to answer back, *Fine, daddy. They're paying me to write about your life.*

From *The Autobiography of a Jukebox*

(1997)

I'm a Fool to Love You

Some folks will tell you the blues is a woman,
Some type of supernatural creature.
My mother would tell you, if she could,
About her life with my father,
A strange and sometimes cruel gentleman.
She would tell you about the choices
A young black woman faces.
Is falling in with some man
A deal with the devil
In blue terms, the tongue we use
When we don't want nuance
To get in the way,
When we need to talk straight?
My mother chooses my father
After choosing a man
Who was, as we sing it,
Of no account.
This man made my father look good,
That's how bad it was.
He made my father seem like an island
In the middle of a stormy sea,
He made my father look like a rock.
And is the blues the moment you realize
You exist in a stacked deck,
You look in a mirror at your young face,
The face my sister carries,
And you know it's the only leverage
You've got?
Does this create a hurt that whispers,
How you going to do?

Is the blues the moment
You shrug your shoulders
And agree, a girl without money
Is nothing, dust
To be pushed around by any old breeze?
Compared to this,
My father seems, briefly,
To be a fire escape.
This is the way the blues works
Its sorry wonders,
Makes trouble look like
A feather bed,
Makes the wrong man's kisses
A healing.

Almost Grown

My father loves my sister so much he has to strike her. He cares
for her so deeply that he has crossed, for the first and only time,
into my mother's domain.

He has caught his daughter red-handed at the front door, try-
ing to sneak home late from her boyfriend's house.

And my father, poor ghost, knows too much. Without ever
leaving the house, he has overheard every sweet thing this man,
an old buddy of his, has whispered to her in bed.

Tonight, my sister discovers her only power. As she tussles
with him on the front porch, she is all heat and righteous passion.

He will never try this hard again to tell anyone how much he loves them. With his belt, my father tries to tell my sister what he knows a man is capable of, but all he does is tell her fortune.

Leavin' Trunk

He's sitting in a car, watching my sister's house, the man who's trying to dog my sister down. Old, and toothless, he's the man who helps her to pay her bills.

And my sister's sick of it, sick and tired of living the way she does, and she's beginning to wonder if there isn't something better she can do with the rest of her life. She's in her early forties. She's beginning to think about moving back home.

She's tired of Mr. Pitiful, who wants too much for his bottom dollar. He watches the house. He spooks her steps. His face is at her bedroom window.

My sister's dreaming of making a midnight creep, of leaving him, a sucker with a mule to ride. She wants the rails to sing of her getaway, no traces left when he pushes open her front door.

And though it'll turn out she's only trading one bad man for another, for my father, who keeps on ice the file of all the things she ought to have done right, in her mind she closes the books, packs her trunk, to see if there's any way in this life to earn a dollar a man can't touch.

Santa Claus (come straight to the ghetto)

It is Christmas Eve, and my good sense won't speak to me. A woman has flagged me down to beg for money for food, and I have stopped at night in my old neighborhood and rolled down the electric window of my rental car.

It is the night before Christmas, and I refuse to listen to the obvious. The doors are power-locked, the engine is in gear and running. Though it is snowing I have clear visibility in the mirror. I decide I can handle this.

And had I been wrong that night, had a gun suddenly appeared from under her coat, had a friend moved from a blind spot into my face, who in the world would have understood? Not the cops, not my family and friends, not my wife, set a-grieving by a whim. Not a soul could have answered *Why the hell did he stop?*

Nothing happens, but I have made a mistake. This is not compassion as she rolls down her sleeve in answer to a question I never ask; as she takes my idiot money and runs as fast as she can away from my car and the shops on Main Street, toward everything I have given her.

Why Was I Born? A Duet Between
John Coltrane & Kenny Burrell

So why? Asks the guitar(ist),
And the sax(ophonist),
A genius, a lover,
Sidesteps the question,
Blows a kiss instead.
Then they both begin to speak
Like bourbon being poured
Into a glass at
Which bar? The eternal one
Bathed in the open light
Of the test pattern, the one
Where the phone booths
Are all functional, but
So? Better here than
Your shitty apartment,
His/Her scent on the
Bedsheets until washday,
Perhaps longer. Better here
Than finding lipstick
On a bathroom glass, his
Brand of cigarette on the dresser.
Their melody is the touch you now wish
You'd never learned, the caress
Of fingers and breath
That promised, promised. What
Hurts is beautiful, the bruise
Of the lyric.

Photo of Miles Davis at
Lennie's-on-the-Turnpike, 1968

New York grows
Slimmer
In his absence.
I suppose

You could also title this picture
Of Miles, his leathery
Squint, the grace
In his fingers a sliver of the stuff

You can't get anymore,
As the rest of us wonder:
What was the name
Of the driver

Of that truck? And the rest
Of us sigh:
Death is one hell
Of a pickpocket.

Chuck Berry

Hamburger wizard,
Loose-limbed instigator,
V-8 engine, purring for a storm

The evidence of a tight skirt, viewed from
    the window of a moving city bus,
Yelling her name, a spell, into the glass.
The amazing leap, from nobody to stockholder,
(*Look, Ma, no hands*), piped through a hot amp.

Figure skater on the rim of the invisible class wall,
The strength of the dreamer who wakes up, and it's
    Monday, a week of work, but gets out of bed

The unsung desire of the checkout clerk.
The shops of the sleepy backwater town,
    waiting for the kid to make good,
        to chauffeur home

The twang of the New Jersey Turnpike
    in the wee, wee hours.
The myth of the lover as he passes, blameless,
    through the walls.

The fury hidden in the word *almost*.
The fury hidden in the word *please*.

The dream of one's name in lights,
Of sending the posse on the wrong trail,
Shaking the wounded Indian's hand, a brother.
. . .

The pulse of a crowd, knowing that the police
Have pushed in the door, dancing regardless

The frenzy of the word *go*.
The frenzy of the word *go*.
The frenzy of the word *go*.

The spark between the thought of the kiss
and receiving the kiss,
The tension in these words:
You Can't Dance.

The amazing duck walk.
The understanding that all it's going to take
    is one fast song.

The triumph in these words:
    Bye-bye, New Jersey, as if rising
    from a shallow grave.

The soda jerk who plots doo-wop songs,
The well-intentioned Business School student
    who does what she's told, suspects
    they're keeping it hid.

Mr. Rock-n-Roll-jump-over
    (or get left behind),
Mr. Taxes? Who, me? Money beat,
Money beat, you can't catch me,
    (but they do),
. . .

A perpetual well of quarters in the pocket.
The incalculable hit of energy in the voice
    of a 16-year-old as her favorite band
    hits the stage,

And 10,000 pairs of eyes look for what they're after:
    More.
And 10,000 voices roar for it:
    More.

And a multitude you wouldn't care to count
    surrounds the joint, waits for the opportunity
    to break in.

Youngblood

I'm sitting in a restaurant, having a very serious discussion with my niece on an Eastern religion, when suddenly, out of the corner of my eyes, I notice the way a young woman crosses the street.

Oh, look at the way she walks as she tries on for size what appears to be a new hairdo for her, a white woman with dreadlocks. She's announcing the changes to a friend who sits waiting for her on a trash can.

And she stops just before she reaches the curb, bends her head low like a wild mare and shakes her new look, tossing the braids aloft like strange, intelligent rope.

How like the woman I used to read about in Richard Brautigan's books, the young spirit with the power to postpone a man from whatever he was thinking, urge him to wipe his glasses to get a closer look.

I'm thinking of him right now, as this woman speaks young
we're-hanging-out-on-a-summer's-afternoon things to her girl-
friend, and they cross back, leaving the afternoon alert and softly
wobbling on its axis.

A Small Moment

I walk into the bakery next door
To my apartment. They are about
To pull some sort of toast with cheese
From the oven. When I ask:
What's that smell? I am being
A poet, I am asking

What everyone else in the shop
Wanted to ask, but somehow couldn't;
I am speaking on behalf of two other
Customers who wanted to buy the
Name of it. I ask the woman
Behind the counter for a percentage
Of her sale. Am I flirting?
Am I happy because the days
Are longer? Here's what

She does: She takes her time
Choosing the slices. "I am picking
Out the good ones," she tells me. It's
April 14th. Spring, with five to ten
Degrees to go. Some days, I feel my duty;
Some days, I love my work.

The Cab Driver Who Ripped Me Off

That's right, said the cab driver,
Turning the corner to the
Roundabout way,
Those stupid, fuckin' beggars,
You know, the guys who
Walk up to my cab
With their hands extended
And their little cups?
You know their problem?
You know what's wrong with them?
They ain't got no brains.
I mean, they don't know nothin',
'cause if they had brains
They'd think of a way
To find a job.
You know what one of 'em told me once?
He said what he did,
Begging,
He said it was work.
Begging
Was work.
And I told him
Straight to his face:
That ain't work.
You think that's work?
Let me tell you what work is:
Work is something that you do
That's of value
To someone else.
Now you take me.

It takes brains to do
What I do.
You know what I think?
I think they ought to send
All these beggars over
To some other country,
Any country,
It don't matter which,
For 3, 4 years,
Let them wander around
Some other country,
See how they like that.
We ought to make a
National program
Sending them off
To wander about
Some other country
For a few years,
Let 'em beg over there,
See how far it gets them.
I mean, look at that guy
You know, who was big
In the sixties,
That drug guy,
Timothy Leary?
Yeah, he went underground,
Lived overseas.
You know what?
A few years abroad
And he was ready to
Come back
On any terms.

He didn't care if
They arrested him.
He said
The U.S. is better
Than any country
In the world.
Send them over there
For a few years.
They'd be just like him.
This is the greatest country
In the whole world.
Timothy Leary
Was damn happy
To get back here,
And he's doing fine.
Look at me.
I used to be like that.
I used to live underground.
I came back.
I think all those beggars got
        a mental block.
I think you should do something.
I mean, you ought to like
        what you do,
But you should do something
Something of use
To the community.
All these people,
Those bums,
Those scam artists,
Those hustlers,
Those drug addicts,

Those welfare cheats,
Those sponges.
Other than that
I don't hold nothin'
Against no one.
Hey, I picked you up.

From *Brutal Imagination*

(2001)

Brutal Imagination

The speaker is the young, nonexistent black man Susan Smith claimed kidnapped her children.

How I Got Born

Though it's common belief
That Susan Smith willed me alive
At the moment
Her babies sank into the lake

When called, I come.
My job is to get things done.
I am piecemeal.
I make my living by taking things.

So now a mother needs me clothed
In hand-me-downs
And a knit cap.

Whatever.
We arrive, bereaved
On a stranger's step.
Baby, they weep,
Poor child.

My Heart

Susan Smith has invented me because
Nobody else in town will do what
She needs me to do.
I mean: jump in an idling car
And drive off with two sad and

Frightened kids in the back.
Like a bad lover, she has given me a poisoned heart.
It pounds both our ribs, black, angry, nothing but business.
Since her fear is my blood
And her need part mythical,
Everything she says about me is true.

Who Am I?

Who are you, mister?
One of the boys asks
From the eternal backseat,
And here is the one good thing:
If I am alive, then so, briefly, are they,
Two boys returned, three and one,
Quiet and scared, bunched together
Breathing like small beasts.
They can't place me, yet there's
Something familiar.
Though my skin and sex are different, maybe
It's the way I drive
Or occasionally glance back
With concern,
Maybe it's the mixed blessing
Someone, perhaps circumstance,
Has given us,
The secret thrill of hiding,
Childish, in plain sight,
Seen, but not seen,

As if suddenly given the power
To move through walls,
To know every secret without permission.
We roll sleepless through the dark streets, but inside
The cab is lit with brutal imagination.

Sightings

A few nights ago
A man swears he saw me pump gas
With the children
At a convenience store
Like a punch line you get the next day,
Or a kiss in a dream that returns while
You're in the middle of doing
Something else.

I left money in his hand.

Mr. ____, who lives in ____,
South Carolina,
Of average height
And a certain weight
Who may or may not
Believe in any of the
Basic recognized religions,
Saw me move like an angel
In my dusky skin
And knit hat.

. . .

Perhaps I looked him in the eye.

Ms. _____ saw a glint of us
On which highway?
On the street that's close
To what landmark?

She now recalls
The two children in the back
Appeared to be behaving.

Mr. _____ now knows he heard
The tires of the car
Everyone is looking for
Crush the gravel
As I pulled up,
In the wee, wee hours
At the motel where
He works the night desk.

I signed or didn't sign the register.
I took or didn't take the key from his hand.
He looked or forgot to look
As I pulled off to park in front
Of one of the rooms at the back.

Did I say I was traveling with kids?
Who slept that night
In the untouched beds?

My Face

If you are caught
In my part of town
After dark,
You are not lost;
You are abandoned.

All that the neighbors will tell
Your kin
Is that you should
Have known better.

All they will do
Is nod their heads.
They will feel sorry
For you,

But rules are rules,
And when you were
Of a certain age
Someone pointed
A finger
In the wrong direction

And said:
All they do
Is fuck and drink
All they're good for
Ain't worth a shit.

You recall me now
To the police artist.

It wasn't really my face
That stared back that day,
But it was that look.

Where Am I?

Looking for Michael and Alex means
That the bushes have not whispered,
That the trees hold only shade
That the lake still insists on being a lake.

I flicker from TV to TV. My flyer sits
On their grandmother's easy chair. I hover
Over so many lawns, so many cups of coffee.

I pour from lip to lip. The town blossoms
In yellow ribbons, sprinkled like bread crumbs
Or bait. I crackle from cell phones and shortwave,

I am listened for in alleys. Looking for Michael
And Alex means each car is scanned at the
Drive-thru windows, that sightings are hoped for

At the self-serve pumps. Clerks long for the crook
Of my arm, reaching for diapers and snacks.
So many days I have loped from ear to ear,

From beauty parlor to church. They count the days
Till someone comes back. We've never left.

The Law

I'm a black man, which means,
In Susan's case,
That I pour out of a shadow
At a traffic light,

But I'm also a mother,
Which is why she has me promise,
"I won't hurt your kids,"
Before I drift down the road.

I'm a mother,
Which is why we sing,
Have mercy, come home,
No questions asked.

But I'm black, and we both know
The law.
Who's going to believe
That we had no choice
But to open that door?

Who's going to care
That it was now or
Never,
That there was no time
To unbuckle them,
That it was take the car
Or leave the car?
. . .

I'm black, which means
I mustn't slow down.
I float in forces
I can't always control,

But I'm also a mother,
Which is why
I hope
I'm as good as my word.

One True Thing

I was made to be a driver, but the truth is, I was, from the
Beginning, Susan's admiral. The sheriff suspects
I sped the car into the lake like the christening of a great
Ship. The fact is, momentum has more than one cure.
You should think of a rowboat, a prank of tiny holes drilled
Into the bottom. A fast car hits the water like a wall of brick
And glue. But a car, gently pushed, quieter than a cop's
Imagination, will bob out, fill up, then roll like a leaky can.

Composite

I am not the hero of this piece.
I am only a stray thought, a solution.
But now my face is stuck to lampposts, glued
To plate glass, my forehead gets stapled
To my hat.

I am here, and here I am not.
I am a door that opens, and out walks
No-one-can-help-you.
Now I gaze, straight into your eye,
From bulletin boards, tree trunks.

I am papered everywhere,
A blizzard called
You see what happens?
I turn up when least expected.
If you decide to buy some milk,

If you decide to wash your car,
If you decide to mail a letter,

I might tumbleweed onto a pant leg.
You can stare, and stare, but I can't be found.
Susan has loosed me on the neighbors,
A cold representative,
The scariest face you could think of.

In 1989, in Boston, Charles Stuart killed his pregnant wife and shot him-
self in a scheme to collect insurance money. He told the police the assailant
was a young black male.

Charles Stuart in the Hospital

Susan Smith now knows what
Charles Stuart knew in Boston:
We do quick, but sloppy work.
All these details:

How tall was I? the police asked Charles,
And ask Susan,
But I vary; I seem smaller and taller
After dusk.
What was the tone of my voice?
Did I growl like a hound as I waved
The pistol in their face?
Was I as desperate as a teenaged boy,
Horny for a sweetheart's kiss?

Here's what I told Susan:
"I won't harm your kids."
But if the moment was mine,
Why would I say that?

I sit with her at the station
The way I sat with Charles
At the hospital:
A shadow on the water glass,
Changing hues,
The slant of my nose and eyes.

Depending on the light
And the question.

Charles rocks in bed with the bullet
We gave ourselves.
How far away was I? We never stopped
To think.
We were in a hurry.
In Boston and South Carolina
I was hungry for a car
And didn't much care how I got it.
Deadly impatient, Charles tells the cops,
But if I couldn't be seen,
But why would I do it that way?
Why do wives and children seem to attract me?

I sat with Charles the way I sit
With Susan; like anyone, and no one,
Changing clothes,
Putting on and taking off ski caps,
Curling and relaxing my hair,
Trying hard to become sense.

Uncle Tom in Heaven

My name is mud; let's get that out
Of the way first. I am not a child.
I was made to believe that God
Kept notes, ran a tab on the blows,
So many on one cheek, so many on
The other.

I watch another black man pour from a
White woman's head. I fear
He'll live the way I did, a brute,
A flimsy ghost of an idea. Both
Of us groomed to go only so far.

That was my duty. I'm well aware
Of what I've become; a name
Children use to separate themselves
On a playground. It doesn't matter
To know I'm someone else's lie,

Anything human can slip, and that's enough
To make grown men worry about
Their accent, where their ambition might
Stray. It doesn't help anything to tell you
I was built to be a hammer,
A war cry. Like him, nobody knew me,

But in my prime, I filled the streets, worried
Into the eardrum, scared up thoughts
Of laws and guns. How I would love
Not to be dubious,

. . .

But I am a question whole races spend
Their time trying to answer. My author
Believed in God, and being denied the
Power to hate her,

I watch another black man roam the land,
Dull in his invented hide.

What I'm Made Of

Susan fills our hands with plain objects,
Key, door handle, steering wheel,
But my hands are nothing:
A song you can't remember
The words to,
The button that pops
Off a vest, a comb that
Falls out of a pocket
Or purse.

Susan fills my lungs with air,
But what do I breathe out?
Parchment, ink, low growls, the
Blank gap between words.

Nothing fits upon my back,
Nothing actually catches my eye,
I am hidden and found,
I am North, South, East, West,
My dark skin porous, in-between.

. . .

Susan claims my name is muscle,
Bone, calls me tissue
And sinew, fills in my blank
With the absence of her boys,

But I am water, pebble,
Silt and gravity,
Evidence under her nail.

What the Sheriff Suspects

Each time the town tells the sheriff
To look harder, my nose straightens and
My hair uncurls. I rustle like wind upon
The surface of a lake. I wink just
Below Susan's cheeks.

The sheriff has shuffled my deck all week.
So many miles, so many deeds.
I do not tire. I can't stop driving. I can
Wrangle kids in broad daylight and never
Be seen or heard. I'm not doing this for ransom.
When I'm about, things simply don't add up,

A short distance becomes too large, clocks run amok,
Stop signs change into traffic lights. Now he wonders
Why he's never noticed the way Susan's body can't sit still,
My accent rising from her alibi.

Next of Kin

The black man in town
They thought looked like me,
Without the dreamed-up cap
And wardrobe,

The police have him now.
He sits in a small room.
They turn him this way
And that.

He'll cool there for hours.
How do you think he feels?
I whisper *we're innocent*
Into his ear.

He looks so much like me,
We could be brothers.
Already, folks
May have their doubts:

He's poor enough.
Where has he been?
He has his needs.
What do they know?

Neighbors call him *quiet,*
A new knot of stress
On the tongue.
. . .

It's been a hard week
To be black in Union, S.C.,
A black woman tells a reporter,

The whites aren't civil.
They look at you and then
Reach over and lock
Their doors.

Now he is it.
Susan has lent me
His cheekbones,
His gait.

For a while,
He is as close as
They'll ever get.

What Is Known About
the Abductor

The sheriff reads off a list of things I have not done:
I have not called on the phone. I did not discard the
Children's clothing they found by the highway,

I wasn't the man who robbed a convenience store
In a car the same color as Susan's. I didn't drop
Off the child they found, in Seattle, in a child's
Seat like hers; the baby someone thought they

Heard crying in the woods; not there, none of
My doing.

Bloodhounds cannot catch a whiff of me. Divers
Rake the bottom of John D. Long Lake. I give
Them a snootful of silt. Who am I? Nothing,
Says the sheriff, can be ruled out. A teenaged girl
Sees a man, covered in mud, walk out of the woods.

The heat sensors of the helicopter they send fail
To light my soggy footprints. Nothing can be
Dismissed. A psychic tumbles through a dream.
He nods as the children point everywhere but
In my direction. I am zip, my
Face and reasons an educated guess.
All week, the police computers grind,

But I am that number after the decimal that keeps
Stuttering, won't resolve.

What Isn't Known About
the Abductor

No name, no known jobs or affiliations.
Was I working alone, was someone else
Waiting to help? Did I intend to rob, carjack,
Or kidnap?
. . .

Why won't I stop? Am I afraid, do I think things
Have spun beyond my control? Why won't I
Simply drop the kids off somewhere?

Was I paid to do this? Did Susan promise me
Reward for taking her children?
Did I do anything sexual to her?

Why did I go for that particular car?
What sort of carjacker
Lies in wait on a deserted road?

No age, no preference, no known associates.
How long have I lived? Will I strike again?
Did I grab hold of a random opportunity?

Am I someone who lives in town?
How can I keep moving yet never be seen?
Why us?

Sympathy

The sheriff's too good to be true.
He tries to urge Susan and me to part.
He trusts a friendly cup of coffee will skim me loose,
But we're hard to untangle.
I won't be easy; we know his help
Is poison. He is courting us.
We run a cold sweat

While he waits.
He is too good to be true.
I am not for his ears, Susan knows.
She tries not to weep; he attempts to lean toward us,
We bob together in the god-awful silence.

Confession

There have been days I've almost
Spilled

From her, nearly taken a breath.
Yanked

Myself clean. I've
Trembled

Her coffee cup. I well
Under

Her eyelids. I've been
Gravel

On her mattress. I am
Not

Gone. I am going to
Worm

. . .

My way out. I have
Not

Disappeared. I half
Slide

Between her teeth,
Double

Her over as she tries
Not

To blurt me out. The
Closer

Susan inches me
Toward

This, the
Louder

The sheriff
Hears

Me bitch.

The italicized language is from Susan Smith's handwritten confession.

Birthing

When I left my home on Tuesday, October 25, I
was very emotionally distraught

I have yet
To breathe.

I am in the back of her mind,
Not even a notion.

A scrap of cloth, the way
A man lopes down a street.

Later, a black woman will say:
"We knew exactly who she was describing."

At this point, I have no language,
No tongue, no mouth.

I am not me, yet.
I am just an understanding.

     *

As I rode and rode and rode, I felt
Even more anxiety.

Susan parks on a bridge,
And stares over the rail.
Below her feet, a dark blanket of river

She wants to pull over herself,
Children and all.

I am not the call of the current.

She is heartbroken.
She gazes down,
And imagines heaven.

      *

*I felt I couldn't be a good mom anymore, but I didn't want
my children to grow up without a mom.*

I am not me, yet.
At the bridge,
One of Susan's kids cries,
So she drives to the lake,
To the boat dock.

I am not yet opportunity.

      *

*I had never felt so lonely
And so sad.*

Who shall be a witness?
Bullfrogs, water fowl.

      *

*When I was at John D. Long Lake
I had never felt so scared
And unsure.*

. . .

I've yet to be called.
Who will notice?
Moths, dragonflies,
Field mice.

*

I wanted to end my life so bad
And was in my car ready to
Go down that ramp into
The water

My hand isn't her hand
Panicked on the
Emergency brake.

*

And I did go part way,
But I stopped.

I am not Gravity,
The water lapping against
The gravel.

*

I went again and stopped.
I then got out of the car.

Susan stares at the sinking.
My muscles aren't her muscles,
Burned from pushing.
The lake has no appetite,
But it takes the car slowly,
Swallow by swallow, like a snake.

*

Why was I feeling this way?
Why was everything so bad
In my life?

Susan stares at the taillights
As they slide from here
To hidden.

*

I have no answers
To these questions.

She only has me,
After she removes our hands
From our ears.

Cornelius Eady is currently director of the Creative Writing Program and an associate professor of English at the University of Notre Dame. He has served as director of the Poetry Center at the State University of New York at Stony Brook and Writer-in-Residence at the College of William & Mary and Sweet Briar College, and he was a member of the guest poetry faculty at New York University and the New School. Eady has also held academic positions at American University, the City College of New York, George Washington University, the University of Alabama at Tuscaloosa, and Sarah Lawrence College. He has taught poetry workshops at the 92nd Street Y and has been on the poetry faculty at Bread Loaf, the National Book Foundation's Summer Writing Camp, and the Community of Writers at Squaw Valley.

Eady's many honors include the Academy of American Poets' Lamont Prize and fellowships from the Rockefeller, Lila Wallace–Reader's Digest, and John Simon Guggenheim foundations; his previous collection, *Brutal Imagination,* was a National Book Award finalist in 2001. "Handymen," one of his new poems, was originally published in *The New Yorker* and will appear in *The Best American Poetry 2008,* edited by Charles Wright. In addition to poetry, Eady is the author of three music-dramas with Deidre Murray: *Running Man*, which was a Pulitzer Prize finalist in 1999 (and of the three finalists, the only music-theater work to be honored), and *You Don't Miss Your Water* and *Brutal Imagination*, based on his poetry collections.

Widely anthologized, Eady is the author of seven other volumes of poetry. He is a cofounder (with the poet Toi Derricotte) and vice president of Cave Canem, which offers workshops, retreats, and other resources to African-American poets.